DOES THE TRIGGER PULL THE FINGER?

THE USES, ABUSES, AND RATIONAL REFORM OF FIREARMS LAW IN THE UNITED KINGDOM

THE SPITFIRE PRESS

RICHARD LAW & PETER BROOKESMITH

Richard Law and Peter Brookesmith are long-standing collaborators
—they co-authored *The Fighting Handgun*, published by
Arms & Armour Press in 1997, and still in print. Richard also
contributed to Peter's *Sniper* (St Martin's Press, 2001: one of the few
books on the subject to analyse the psychology of the job).
Both have written for various shooting magazines including
Guns Review, *Guns and Shooting*, *Target Gun*, and *Handgunner*. and
currently edit and contribute to *The Shooter's Journal*.
Both are graduates of the Lethal Force Institute of New Hampshire
and consider themselves to be not entirely inexpert shots; they have
also devised various competitive shooting courses and instructed
both tyros and experienced shots in various shooting disciplines.

Richard Law is a recognized expert witness on questions of firearms
law, history and technical matters, and has been secretary of the
Shooter's Rights Association since 1985.
Apart from his books on firearms and their practical applications,
Peter Brookesmith has published an eclectic series of titles on
subjects ranging through alien abductions, plagues and diseases, and
the care, feeding, and psychology of horses.

RICHARD LAW
& PETER BROOKESMITH

DOES THE TRIGGER
PULL THE FINGER?

THE USES, ABUSES, AND RATIONAL REFORM
OF FIREARMS LAW IN THE UNITED KINGDOM

THE SPITFIRE PRESS

Does the Trigger Pull the Finger?
An Original Publication of The Spitfire Press
An imprint of FireCrest International Limited

First published in April 2011 by FireCrest International Ltd
Llanerchymeidwy, Llwyndrain, Llanfyrnach, Pembrokeshire, Wales

Cover image: iStock Photo
Cover design: Mick Cathcart
Typography and typesetting: Peter Brookesmith

A CIP catalogue record for this book is available from the British Library

ISBN: 978-1-906174-99-6

Printed and bound in the UK by Lightning Source UK Ltd, Milton Keynes,
and in the USA by Lightning Source Inc, LaVergne, Tennessee

*Laws are dangerous to everyone, innocent and guilty alike, because they have
no human understanding in and of themselves. They must be interpreted.*
—Brian Herbert & Kevin J Anderson

*The threat of people acting in their own enlightened and rational self-interest
strikes bureaucrats, politicians and social workers as ominous and dangerous.*
—W. G. Hill

As government expands, liberty contracts.
—Ronald Reagan

*If someone has a gun and is trying to kill you, it would be reasonable
to shoot back with your own gun.*
—Tenzin Gyatso, the 14th Dalai Lama

CONTENTS

INTRODUCTION
NONE SO BLIND

CONTRARY TO LEGEND, the United Kingdom is awash with firearms: we estimate there are well in excess of 20 million of them in the country. That figure doesn't include the countless antiques left over from our military past and sporting heritage, but it does include those currently in use by the armed forces and the police, target-shooting clubs and youth organizations, farmers and slaughtermen, wildfowlers and countrymen.

There's also a huge number not in use. They are sitting in cupboards and drawers, safety deposit boxes and trunks, in military and police armouries and stores, hanging on walls in castle and cottages, hiding under thick grease and thin cement, on display in gunshops.

Of those 20 million firearms, some 10 percent are registered to individual users on firearm and shotgun certificates. It's a tiny minority of the metal that's out there yet, every time Parliament or one of its McCarthyite select committees considers 'firearms', it's that tiny minority of legally registered weapons that they obsess about.

And, note, it's usually those inanimate items of precision engineering that preoccupy them—not the people who lawfully own and use them. Nearly every time, in the UK, that something goes horribly wrong and there's a firearm involved, one kind of gun or another is 'banned'—made difficult or impossible for people to register as lawfully owned.

New York attorney Jeffrey R. Snyder has remarked on the moral inversion embedded in this approach:

> [T]o ban guns because criminals use them is to tell the innocent and law-abiding that their rights and liberties depend not on their own conduct, but *on the conduct of the guilty and the lawless*, and that the law will permit them to have only such rights and liberties as *the lawless will allow*. ...For society does not control crime, ever, by forcing the law-abiding to accommodate themselves to the expected behavior of criminals. Society

controls crime by forcing the criminals to accommodate themselves to the expected behavior of the law-abiding.*

The government's inverted thinking was all too clear to the 10,000-odd owners of semi-automatic fullbore rifles who had *not* misused their personal property but were deprived of it because Michael Ryan went on a murderous spree in 1987, and equally plain to 57,000 or so innocent shooters who lost their handguns after Thomas Hamilton ran amok in 1996. The injustice was all the more deeply felt because these prohibitions had no hope of preventing or deterring any repetition of such an appalling crime in the future. The one thing we know about spree killers is that they are not predictable, as Derrick Bird— known as a friendly, popular, good-humoured man, 'a laugh'—cruelly demonstrated in the summer of 2010. To put the injustice in Snyder's terms, the law-abiding were being forced to accommodate themselves to the depradations of the deranged.

And on top of that, the government was paying no attention to all those other firearms, at least 5 million of which are in private hands, that have never been registered, and which feature rarely in crime. One couldn't escape the impression that the powers-that-be were lazily picking on the people it was easiest to pick on.

A law unto themselves

That is certainly the picture that shooters generally have of the police, who administer the law. It is, as a matter of statistics, an erroneous impression: most police firearms management officers are fair and reasonable, and strive personfully to assist firearm and shotgun certificate applicants and holders in navigating the treacherous waters of the relevant law. But, as the accounts of various court cases scattered throughout this book show, some are none of the kind, and behave with what we can only call an obsessive-compulsive pedantry, or worse: we know of one officer who proudly boasted to a certificate holder: "We can do what we like when it comes to firearms." Such an outlook brings semi-surreal prosecutions to court in its wake and, ultimately, as such cases accumulate, the law into disrepute.

A classic instance was *Regina v. Chelmsford Crown Court, ex parte Farrer* in 2000. Arthur Mark Farrer, a Deputy Lord Lieutenant of Essex and practising solicitor and thus, we may assume, not inclined to criminal habits, put in for a renewal of his shotgun certificate. In due course a policeman arrived at the cottage on Mr Farrer's estate

* Jeff Snyder, "Who's Under Assault in the 'Assault Weapon' Ban?", *American Rifleman*, October 1994, p53. [Emphases have been added.]

where both his shotguns and his 81-year-old mother lived. The officer wanted to inspect Mr Farrer's security and check the guns against the details on his renewal application. Mrs Farrer obligingly opened the gun safe for him, as she happened to know where the keys were. When this shocking news reached the ears of the chief constable of Essex—or, more likely, those of his firearms manager—he refused to renew Mr Farrer's ticket on the grounds that he allowed unauthorized access to his guns (Mrs Farrer had no certificate of her own).

Mr Farrer tried negotiating with the chief constable, got nowhere, and appealed to the Crown Court, which upheld the chief constable's view. A judicial review followed, and finally the matter landed up in the Court of Appeal. Which decided that "the practical convenience of Mrs Farrer having access, and the general good sense in having a wife or close relative able (as in this case) to facilitate police inspection or permit removal in case of fire or the demise of the certificate holder, was outweighed by the strict wording of the Act."

Perhaps the court was correct on the strict point of law. However, it seems to have overlooked two other points of law, as did the police. First, the police were acting *ultra vires* in inspecting Mr Farrer's security arrangements, since the law gives them no such authority. Second, the only legal grounds for not renewing Mr Farrer's certificate would be that he posed a danger to public safety. That danger amounted to his unauthorized mother having access to his guns. We do have to wonder if an 81-year-old lady of impeccable character is really all that likely to turn into a Hell's Granny.

'Twas ever thus, from childhood's hour

The real problem here is not so much the nit-picking failure of "general good sense" (as the court put it) on the part of Essex police, ridiculous as that is, as that the police have the power both to grant *and to revoke* firearm and shotgun certificates solely on their own authority. This conflicts with the Human Rights Act 1998, European case law (*McGonnell v. United Kingdom* 2000) and natural justice: and it leaves the injured party having, in effect, to prove his own innocence in any appeal. Such an arrangement, unique in British law, is wide open to abuse, as we shall see. Worse, it's underwritten by guidance to the police that manages to ignore most of the relevant case law and, on occasion, the letter of the law itself. As we shall also see, the kind of prosecution (or persecution) represented here by the Farrer case has little to do with preventing real crime by real criminals.

Not that crime, as committed by criminals, has ever featured much in the government's nervousness about guns. The 1920 Firearms Act, which required *new* purchases of handguns from firearms dealers to be registered, was introduced in the hope of deterring would-be revolutionaries from turning the UK into a Bolshevik state. The revolution never did occur, but millions of people also never bothered to register the pistols they'd owned before the Act was passed. An Act in 1937 made it illegal to buy (but not to own) machine guns, for no reason that we can discern other than that they'd become popular with American gangsters—no one in this country had used one in the course of a crime (we discount the politically-motivated insurgents of the Irish Republican Army, who'd in any case achieved most of their objectives 15 years previously). The 1968 Firearms Act, which created the legal definitions of firearms types that we still use, was a consolidating act, whose requirement to register shotguns had been a response to the murder in 1966 of three policemen by criminals wielding *pistols*. These were, in essence, laws passed in reaction to non-existent problems. The 1988 and 1997 Acts were knee-jerk reactions to insoluble problems.

Running amok with a rifle

This is not a book about spree killers (although we could write one) but about the uselessness, misguidedness and maladministration of current firearms law in the UK—and its rational reformulation, in a fashion that would both bring more guns into a system of controls, and almost certainly improve public safety and enhance the serenity of the Queen's peace. Nonetheless it's important to make a couple of points about spree killers, besides the one that all policemen and criminologists know: that they're detectable only *once they've started to kill.*

There seems to be an assumption, or a wilful ignorance, in certain quarters, that spree killers are exceptionally fond of firearms. And therefore, the logic runs, spree killers will be stopped in their tracks if you keep them away from guns or, better yet, remove guns from everyone but soldiers and policemen lest someone go bananas one day. Apart from making all those 'everyones' incapable of defending themselves and others from attack, the syllogism is false from the get-go. Let's first take the notion that if only the police and the military had legal access to firearms, potential spree killers might sweat things out at home, not take to the streets with murderous intent.

Kenya has somewhat more stringent gun laws than the UK: anyone convicted of possessing an unauthorized firearm faces the death penalty. And in practice, few people outside various government services such as the military, national park rangers, and the police do own guns. On 5 November 2010, no one expected Peter Karanja, a constable in Kenya's security police, to leave his post outside the District Commissioner's house in Siakago, and go from bar to bar shooting people who had the bad luck not to know where he could find his girlfriend who, he believed, was up to no good with another man. Ten people died, including two police colleagues who tried to intervene. Karanja then turned his Heckler & Koch G3 rifle on himself, but had run out of ammunition. He proceeded to Siakago police station and turned himself in.

The moral, unfortunately, is that policemen are no more predictable, or safe, than anyone else. For those interested in curious facts, the record for spree killings with a firearm is held by a policeman, one Woo Bum-kon, who in April 1982 slaughtered about 62 people in Uiryeong, South Korea, before killing himself with a hand grenade.

Gun-free sprees—from Kenya to Texas

As we noted, relatively few people in Kenya own guns, not least because most cannot afford one, let alone the bribes required to process a license application successfully. So in April 2004 Jamin Mukobero Muchika used a *panga* (a form of machete—in other words, an agricultural implement) to slaughter his pregnant wife, four children, one nephew and two sisters-in-law. He also attacked seven other members of his unhappy family, who survived, before trying and failing to remove himself from the scene by swallowing pesticide.

In August 1993, an unidentified Kenyan mowed down 43 people (more than just one bus queue), of whom 18 died, in Kilifi, with his car—in which he made good his escape.

Firearms in private hands are virtually unknown in Japan, a country often held up as a model by members of the gun-control lobby. In December 2010, reported the London *Times*, "A man wielding a 25cm (10in) kitchen knife attacked passengers on two crowded buses in Toride near Tokyo, before he was overpowered. He wounded 14 passengers, who were mostly schoolchildren."

New York City has such draconian gun-control laws that only cops, robbers, and the rich have firearms. In Brooklyn on 12 February 2011, Maksim Gelman, a 23-year-old of Ukrainian birth, fatally stabbed his stepfather, the mother of a girl who'd turned down his advances, and the girl herself. Gelman then drove off, crashed into another car and stabbed the driver, who survived. He next drove into a pedestrian, who later died in hospital. Then he hailed a cab and stabbed the driver, who survived. Next Gelman hijacked a car, stabbing its owner in the hand. At some point he took to the subway, and hacked at a passenger before finally being subdued by police at Times

Square station. New York's police commissioner Raymond Kelly told the press that he "had never encountered such a bloody spree" in all his decades on the force.

The following day, in Sayreville, New Jersey, William Pittel, aged 58 and homeless, bought a cup of coffee at the Burger King on 960 Route 9 South, then stabbed three elderly customers with a 6in-long steak knife. He ran off, but was soon picked up in a nearby pizza shop. Police said there was no apparent motive. All three victims survived the attack.

Unlike New York City, the State of Texas is not renowned for its hostility toward firearms ownership. Andrew Joseph Stack III, aged 53, of Austin could have gone to a licensed dealer and bought any amount of firepower short of a machine gun on producing a Texas driving licence as ID. After years of acrimonious disputes with (and festering hatred of) the federal Internal Revenue Service (IRS), Stack's boiler blew on 18 February 2010. He set fire to his house, drove 20 miles to Georgetown municipal airport, and took off in his Piper Dakota light aircraft. About 10 minutes later he flew it directly into Echelon I, an Austin office block in which 190 IRS officials worked. The plane, which Stack had laden with fuel, turned into a fireball. One taxman died, and 13 others were injured. One may take it that Stack had hoped to take more with him when he died.

The cases recounted above are the murderous gun-free sprees that we happened to come across just while working on this book. No doubt there have been many more. But we think we make our point.

Politicians jump in—a little too soon

In 2000 and 2010 the Home Affairs Select Committee of the House of Commons took it upon themselves to consider whether the system of firearms controls in the UK could be improved. In 2000, the new régime introduced in the 1997 Amendment Act had barely had time to bed in. In autumn 2010, they were hoping 'something could be *done*' after Derrick Bird's rampage earlier in the year. Neither an official enquiry into whether Bird's certificates had been properly authorized (by a Dorset Assistant Chief Constable, set up by Cumbria police), nor another, under the auspices of ACPO, into police operations to counter him, had reported when the Committee announced its own enquiry, so it too seemed premature. In both cases the Committee's cast of mind was apparent from its language: it was after more controls.

This no doubt explains their fascination, in their 2010 report, for the rigmarole that people have to go through if they want to register a handgun in Washington DC. Fingerprints and photographs are taken, ballistic samples are taken from the pistol, and many dollars go into the public coffers. This obstructive process (or bureaucratic job-creation scheme) is currently the subject of an appeal to the US Supreme Court, but that's not the thickest of the ironies here.

Peter Nickles, the Attorney General of Washington DC, was able to assure the Committee that registered firearms featured not at all in crime, thus, we assume, bolstering their notion that registration—or 'licensing', as they insisted on calling it—was *ipso facto* a good thing. What he didn't tell them (and the Committee's report omits it too) was the background to DC's handgun registration scheme. In 1976, DC made it impossible to register handguns, in effect banning them or, to put it another way, relinquishing control of them. Pragmatic residents simply acquired pistols in neighbouring States, either to use in pursuit of their criminal careers or for defending their homes and persons. In due course, a federal security guard, Richard Heller, decided to challenge DC's restrictive régime and requested a permit to keep the Colt .45ACP he used for work at home, for self-defence. The city declined his request. Heller and his supporters took the view that the decision infringed his constitutional rights under the Second Amendment ("...the right of the people to keep and bear arms..."), and applied to a federal court for a ruling.

We can still teach those colonials a thing or two

The case worked its way up to the US Supreme Court (SCOTUS), which delved well beyond the Second Amendment *and into the English common law on which it is founded* and, in June 2008, published its decision. That established that the right to keep and bear arms is an *individual* right, and that DC's pistol ban was unconstitutional. The following December, the city passed a Firearms Registration Emergency Amendment Act to comply with the SCOTUS judgement.

By mid 2010, 1200-odd people had registered handguns for home defence. That these guns didn't appear in crime is probably no more than a reflection of the very short period the system had been in place, although Peter Nickles kept quiet about that, just as he failed to mention that the registration scheme was a relaxation, not a tightening, of firearms law in DC. Not unexpectedly, but contrary to the predictions of the city's Mayor, what he called 'handgun violence' had also decreased over the same period. Dire prophesies that the streets will run with blood and vigilantism will flourish are cried up every time a US jurisdiction 'relaxes' its gun controls, but have never come to pass. The general trend, as in DC, is that armed criminals, no longer certain as to which potential victims are armed and which are not, decide to exercise a degree of prudence and caution when conducting their business. (See the Appendix for more on this.) We should in fairness note, too, that violent crime as a whole in the US, as in the UK, has been in decline since the early Noughties.

We deal with other lacunæ, in their thinking and their questions, in the Select Committee's enquiries of 2000 and 2010, in Chapter Nine. Overall, our impression remains that—although their chairman has a degree in law—the Committee were patently unaware of the relevant law and the cavalier manner in which it's treated by both the Home Office and the police, and (like both those vested interests) were fixated on the hardware rather than the people who own it.

This was particularly apparent in their rabbiting on about imitation weapons, de-activated guns and blank firers, which by definition are not firearms and in any case rarely cause problems. We were impressed that their statistics found that in 2008/9, *imitation* firearms had somehow been fired 1067 times, causing death or serious injury on 14 occasions; after that we were inclined to think that their tables of numbers didn't mean much. We were impressed too by the attention they gave to the Gun Control Network, a shadowy organization of fully four members, with a talent for spinning figures. On the whole, the Committee succeeded in missing the point whenever they could. If they did do any homework, their dog had surely eaten it by the time they went into session.

The structure of this book

We did agree with one Select Committee recommendation, iterated in 2000 and in 2010, that the UK's firearms laws desperately need to be simplified. This book offers a rather neat way to do just that.

Part One covers the deep background: after a general survey of the way things are, in Chapter One, we rehearse the history of common law and firearms legislation in the UK as it developed from King Alfred's time, up to the end of the Second World War. If you're not aware of the common law and its implications, or want to take an obscure masochistic pleasure from observing how coarsely the mills of bureaucracy can grind, read this.

Otherwise, move straight to Part Two (page 45), which deals with the birth and development of the law we have today, and the interesting way in which the police administer it. Here we cover policy and legislation from about 1965 through to the Home Office Select Committee's hearings in 2000 and 2010. Much of what's in this part seems to be beyond the grasp of the national shooting organizations *and* the gun-control lobby, so we especially commend it to both. If you can't bear the prospect, move straight to page 85, where—

Part Three sets out how we think a real balance can be struck between the government's incurable yearning to control firearms, and reconciling that with the common law and with human rights legislation, while making everyone safer. We'd start by removing the current prohibitions on handguns, semi-auto centre-fire rifles, *and* fully-automatic weapons. This may strike some as a paradox (and bring others out in hives) because at its heart is the idea that more people should register guns, be they pistols or AK-47s, and that the police should have as little as possible to do with the process. This is not as mad, bad and dangerous as some may think. We know that at least 90 percent of the firearms in the country are not registered. Our system, using a national database administered by an independent agency, would make most of them legal and trackable, creating an official record that presently does not exist. As for the police: they have disgraced themselves by abusing their present powers, and their business should be restricted to catching real criminals, not bullying sand harassing people who've shown they are keen to stay within the law.

Whether people use their guns or not is another matter. Not everyone will want to. We have ways of dealing fairly with both these classes of interested parties, too, and effective ways of keeping dodgy characters at more than arm's length from guns—ways that *might* have prevented the three spree killings the UK has seen in the last quarter-century. In any case, guns should be kept securely. These aspects of keeping and bearing arms can be administered by people who, unlike the police, won't be a burden on the public purse and who will have real, not abstract, knowledge of those concerned.

By the way—if you do read the whole book from cover to cover, you'll find a few points repeated: this is deliberate, and done so that those reading only one part will be *au fait* with certain technicalities.

The Appendix examines the legend that the United States has 'lax' gun laws and whether or not lax or strict firearms controls affect the number of people who die by gunfire in various jurisdictions. It turns out that things aren't quite as simple as some would have you believe.

Back in the UK: we believe that the end result of our proposals would be simplified law, improved public safety, lower costs for the taxpayer, a huge boost to the gun trade—and a general increase in the gaiety of nations, as an ancient demonization of inert pieces of wood, metal and polymers becomes a thing of the past.

Now read on.

PART ONE

THE DEEP BACKGROUND

The right of ordinary citizens to possess weapons is the most extraordinary, most controversial, and least understood of those liberties secured by Englishmen and bequeathed to their American colonists. It lies at the very heart of the relationship between the individual and his fellows, and between the individual and his government.
—Joyce Lee Malcolm

When you disarm your subjects... you offend them by showing that either from cowardliness or lack of faith, you distrust them; and either conclusion will induce them to hate you.
—Niccolo Machiavelli

CHAPTER ONE

IT'S NOT JUST ABOUT GUNS

THREE TIMES in the last quarter-century, the United Kingdom has seen someone go on a murderous rampage with firearms that they had acquired legally and had duly registered. On 19 August 1987, in and around Hungerford, Berkshire, 27-year-old Michael Ryan, carrying two fullbore semi-automatic rifles and a semi-auto handgun, shot 16 people dead (one was his mother), wounded fifteen more, and then shot himself dead. On 13 March 1996, in Dunblane, Scotland, 44-year-old Thomas Hamilton killed 16 primary-school children and their teacher with a handgun—he was carrying four—and wounded about a dozen more, before turning a revolver on himself. On 2 June 2010, 52-year-old Derrick Bird went on a spree around the county of Cumbria with a shotgun and a .22 semi-auto rifle, killing 12 people (the first to die was his twin brother) and wounding 11 others. By the time police caught up with him, he had taken his own life.

Predictably, there were calls in the aftermath of these outrages for the government to '*do something*' that would, ostensibly at least, prevent another incident of the kind. Demands ranged from banning all small arms, of any kind, from private ownership, to 'tightening' the law in some way so that potential spree killers could be spotted before they could obtain guns; or at least before they could obtain them legally. In response, the government of the day duly redefined fullbore semi-auto rifles as 'prohibited weapons' in 1988 (although Ryan had shot more people with his pistol than with his rifles), and in 1997 did the same for handguns.

In 2010, the reaction from on high was less of a knee jerk, as the Prime Minister soon made plain that that wasn't on the cards; and as we go to press there have as yet been no proposals for new legislation. It's just possible too that a gleam of logic may have penetrated the government mind at this point. For within a month of Derrick

Bird's rampage, one Raoul Moat came out of the woodwork—in the shape of Durham Prison—to shoot his former girlfriend's new beau dead, wound her, and blind a policeman; he then tied up the firearms teams of half the police forces of the kingdom as he went on the run for nearly a week. Cornered eventually, he too shot himself dead. But Moat had acquired his sawn-off shotgun not with a firearms certificate, but through the back channels of the underworld. Nothing could have made it plainer, even to the battened-down minds of politicians and civil servants, that someone who wants a firearm badly enough, and has the right contacts, is not going to be trammelled by any law, new or old.

A gun-control lobby emerges—with a vengeance

Thomas Hamilton's grotesque killing spree in 1996 probably caused more uproar than Ryan's had in 1987, and probably because his victims were mainly children—and so many of them. The Conservative government decided to ban fullbore handguns, a move that Home Office officials had first considered as long ago as 1870. The Dunblane murders became their 'suitable legislative opportunity', and cosmetic legislation was the failing, sleaze-ridden government's kiss-off to the voters who, they knew, wouldn't return them anyway.

The incoming Government, who styled themselves 'New Labour', had already flagged up firearms law for further attention. What that might mean they made clear enough, and with transparent cynicism, by choosing Ann Pearston of the Snowdrop Campaign, then the UK's most prominent anti-gun group, as the keynote speaker at their pre-election conference. In opposition, their position during debates on the Conservative Government's 1997 firearms bill was that it wasn't going far enough—which was also the line they had taken on the post-Hungerford firearms bill in 1988. Labour MPs made some quite intemperate remarks in 1997: one said that the assets of shooting clubs should be sequestrated and used to compensate the police for the costs of collecting in all the guns for destruction.

You might think that this is a rather startling attitude, in a public servant, toward the legally-owned private property of the law-abiding electorate he purported to serve. But such was the atmosphere in 1996 and '97. For the Dunblane murders had sent a series of shock waves through British society. First came the numbing horror that everyone felt at such an awful crime. Then came demands for revenge, primarily from the press. They called it justice, but confiscation of personal property without a conviction conflicts with the European Convention on Human Rights. So revenge it was and, for the first time in the United Kingdom, an active gun-control lobby emerged. It was a mixture of bereaved parents seeking retribution and less excusable band-waggoners, but it was a lobby nonetheless. The front runners were the Snowdrop Campaign and the Gun Control Network, along with the Society Against Guns in Europe (which, set up as a charity, was soon exposed as a money-grabbing scam). And they soon had their way: shortly after being elected, the Labour government banned smallbore pistols too. There hadn't been a gun-control lobby in the UK before, as such—because one way or the other the only people interested in restricting the freedom of others were, and still are, government employees.

In two minds: attitudes to self-defence

The sudden emergence of this lobby didn't, and doesn't, seem to reflect public opinion at large. Most people's attitude toward guns might be summarized thus: they may be slightly alarmed on discovering that their neighbours have firearms, then they become a little intrigued by the subject. In our experience, most people who discover they have local access to one of the shooting sports, would like at least to have a go. Various TV programmes looked into firearms ownership in the 1990s, and their telephone polls were usually in favour of the idea of people having guns. Such results do, however, depend on the question. If asked whether they should be allowed an Uzi submachine gun to defend their homes, most people say Yes. If asked whether their neighbour should be allowed to have firearms that they themselves can't own, most people tend to say No.

So: if you're against the idea of *other* people having guns— although you might quite like to have one for your self-defence—any misuse of them can appear at first blush to be evidence that guns should be outlawed. Governments have played on this internal dichotomy of opinion for years.

A significant proportion of the populace would, just the same, prefer to have a robust means of defending life, liberty, chastity and property, and the blessing of statute law in doing so. This became became clear in January 2004, when BBC Radio Four's flagship programme *Today* asked listeners to say what new law they thought would most improve life in modern Britain. Labour MP Stephen Pound volunteered to sponsor a private member's bill enshrining the popular vote. Proposals were whittled down to a shortlist of five, which included such well-meaning ideas as making *post-mortem* organ harvesting compulsory, and banning Christmas-themed advertising before 1 December each year. Of the 26,007 listeners—by definition a representative sample of the population—who voted, 9622, or 37 percent, wanted to see a law that authorized using "any means they saw fit" to defend their homes from intruders. Mr Pound promptly denounced the notion as a "ludicrous, brutal, unworkable blood-stained piece of legislation"—terms measurably more hysterical than those of the proposal itself—and declined to start work on a draft bill. Reporting his embarrassment, the *Independent* headed its article "MP calls Radio 4 listeners 'bastards' over vigilante vote."

Vigilantism, of course, had nothing to do with it, but that wasn't going to stand in the way of a scary headline. No doubt Mr Pound saw the fearsome implication of having such a law: it would make defence of life and property a 'good reason' to acquire registered firearms, regardless of declared Home Office policy. But apart from exposing yet again the patronizing attitudes of our ruling élites, the episode revealed how little people know of their existing, inalienable rights under the common law.

In any case you can't un-invent firearms. In our view, owning one (or two) by and large has a positive effect in maintaining law and order, the safety of the individual, his family and his property, not to mention his nation and government. When things go wrong and get a negative press, they usually go wrong somewhere whose laws make it difficult for the public to own or get access to firearms. On a level playing field, where private individuals may have the same firearms as government employees, the question of ownership just isn't an issue for either the people or their government.

One law for them, another for us

Owning guns becomes a problem when restrictions affect some people but not others. For example, New York City's 1911 Sullivan Act makes it extremely difficult to be both law-abiding and a gun owner, unless you're rich or know an influential politician. The broad effect is that most guns are in the hands of government employees and those who ignore the law: cops and robbers. In places like this, there is usually also a subculture of people who are law-abiding in all respects *apart* from that one law. Such selective behaviour is usually a sign that the law should be looked at again.

Gun owners are not peculiar in that respect; there are plenty of people who use scheduled drugs unlawfully, but don't habitually exceed speed limits, never fail to pay maintenance to their former spouses, and always honour their tax bills. It's when government regulation conflicts more than strictly necessary with what should be individual choices that a lack of conformity emerges, and may become widespread. The man-in-the-street's view is that a ban on buying heroin is general; he can't have it, and neither can government employees. When it comes to firearms, however, the illogicality of a partial ban becomes obvious. Because it's not a ban, as such: it's an administrative device, whereby some public servants have restricted the possession of certain firearms to certain other public servants, while denying them to the public they all claim to serve. Apart from its moral dubiety, such a strategy is not calculated to increase trust between ourselves, and our rulers and those who enforce the rules.

In shooting, much of what we do is practice; but if we haven't learned the right way to do things, those practice sessions are not stepping stones to perfection: they are merely the repetition of error. The same can be said of firearms legislation. Because it set off with the wrong objective, each subsequent re-visit to the subject has built on the errors of the past, repeating and amplifying them, to the point where no one in public administration takes the slightest interest in the consequences of repeating the same mistakes, let alone the advantages of correcting them. Restrictions on owning firearms have gradually become an end in themselves. Our firearms legislation has been mistaken, we say, because its costs—financial, personal, and public—exceed the benefits (if any) we gain in return.

An elephant in the committee room

The two shooting incidents of 2010, hot on the heels of a general election, were nonetheless deemed enough of a mandate for the House of Commons' Home Affairs Select Committee to decide to study firearms legislation and its impact. But it was immediately obvious, from the way the Committee framed its questions and interests, that they weren't concerned with the real problem. They may have been diverted from it by bureaucrats. More likely, they simply hadn't realized there *was* a problem. But it's only when the real problem is clearly identified that one can seek real, workable solutions. And the Committee seemed, in autumn 2010, intent on doing neither.

We thought we could do better. Those of us who have watched the law and its administration develop, have also seen all the intended and unintended consequences, squirmed at the repetition of error, the ignorance of politicians and the duplicity of civil servants and the police. We are also those who have paid the price of media 'justice'.

Hence this book. See what you think.

CHAPTER TWO
LIBERTY AND JUSTICE FOR ALL

HERE IS 2011: more than a century of firearms legislation has affected the law-abiding voters of the United Kingdom—the people who periodically have to don uniforms and sort out with gunfire our government's foreign policy objectives—or failings. The 20th century saw a lot of firearms manufactured for precisely that reason—in support of government policy—and every government has at least one policy that results in firearms being manufactured, stockpiled, and occasionally, sometimes rather grudgingly, handed out to the voters so that they can defend their realm.

The 20th century saw nothing added to the small-arms inventory; there were no new inventions. We entered the 21st century with improved 19th-century firearms technology. Certainly, manufacturing quality and speed improved and materials were enhanced, but in mechanical terms there is nothing on the small-arms market now that you couldn't have bought in 1899. But in 1899 in the UK you could buy all and any of what was available and break no law. A century later, that's difficult or impossible.

That change is the fruit of successive governments' confused approach to making law. Sometimes, in trying to solve one apparent problem, they created another. For example, introducing firearms certificates in 1920 also created a pool of unregistered (and thus untraceable) but not illegal weapons: for the majority of privately-held firearms were already outside the supposed controls.*

The notion of limiting who owned what guns did not spring fully-formed like Athene from the head of Zeus; the idea of 'gun control'

---

* In this book we've avoided using the more common term 'illegal pool' for guns not held on certificates—partly because we suspect that most of them are not actually illegally owned, but also because we want to include weapons held by the police, the military, and other public servants in this category of off-ticket weapons.

has a back-story. The part of that story that has always embarrassed British governments intent on 'gun control' is the common law, so that's where we will begin.

The foundations of the common law

In the ninth century of our common era, Alfred the Great (849-99) set in motion the basis of English law, establishing the concept of what King Henry II at the 1192 Assizes called the common law: that body of what is right and what is wrong that had not been set down in statute. To this day in the UK, murder is a crime contrary to the common law. If you confine yourself to Parliamentary legislation, you will find no statute that outlaws murder.

The common law is a body of common-sense decisions, reinforced and refined by case law, that determine right from wrong, setting out standards of behaviour to which everyone is expected to adhere. In Alfred the Great's time, the basis of the law was the Bible. God handed the Ten Commandments down to Moses, who handed them on down to the people, along with a considerable amount of supporting legislation. But the core standards of behaviour required of people toward one another as set out in the Old Testament held good as the basis for decision-making by the king of England many centuries later. They call upon everyone to respect one another and their property.

As the country became larger and its activities more complex, the business of justice devolved to Lords sitting in judgement, with the King's Assizes sitting as an appellate court. That's why Henry II found himself coining the phrase 'common law': he meant that the law should apply uniformly and equally to all subjects. To that basic law was added other legislation, temporary or permanent, handed down by the King or the church. Most laws cost money to enforce, so passing a law is something that is essentially limited to an authority that has revenue-raising powers. Your golf, darts or shooting club can promulgate laws because it can raise the money to fund its new legislation by adjusting your fees. That example makes it clear that any legislative body can pass only those laws that are relevant to its reason for existence, and its powers are limited to their purpose.

Your club committee's laws regulate the members or their facilities. They can't amend a national organization's laws, for example—because they didn't pass the original law, and they don't have the means or power to enforce their legislation among a population wider than their own members.

Governments are the same. Parliament can only legislate for the people who elected them and they can't amend laws they didn't pass in the first place: so the Ten Commandments are safe. Parliament didn't hand them down to Moses, so Parliament can't amend them. It's also the case that Parliament didn't pass, and therefore can't amend, quite a few of the core documents of our constitution, one of which is the Bill of Rights.

What Parliament can do is legislate to deal with problems that they think can be resolved through their intervention. When motor cars first appeared, Parliament legislated to prevent them alarming other road users (frightening the horses) by requiring that they should be preceded by a pedestrian carrying a red flag. They can also repeal laws of their own or a previous Parliament's making, as they did with the Red Flag Act, when they cease to be relevant.

Throughout our history as a nation, governments have passed laws relating to weapons. Some are familiar to everyone: Edward VI made archery practice on the village green on Sundays compulsory, for example. Swords were—at various times—restricted to people of rank. Gentlemen were the lowest rank in society permitted to wear a sword; mere esquires could not.

As time went by, the weaponry changed. Underwater archaeology on Henry VIII's flagship *Mary Rose* turned up both arrows and a lot of longbows—most of which are too powerful for people to use today! Just a few handguns are mentioned. That was in 1545.

A generation later, the Spanish Armada seems to have had fewer bows and more guns. The Spanish navy seems to have had crossbows, which could be used in wet conditions, but the army on board seem to have been matchlock musketeers. Swords took longer to pass from common use. Portraiture suggests that everyone wore their swords when they sat for artists, until about 1745. A generation later, hardly anyone sits wearing one. But by then people were travelling in coaches on improved roads. A brace of pistols for the gentlemen and blunderbusses for the coachmen were more appropriate in the circumstances than long cutlery. But taking the precaution of going armed against footpads and highwaymen was still the norm.

Now let's rewind a century or so.

God, the gun, and the common law

In the early 17th century religious non-conformists from England began to colonize the eastern seaboard of the Americas. The mid-century saw the English civil war, the puritan Commonwealth government between the reigns of Kings Charles I and II, strife in Ireland, war in Europe directly fermented by the Catholic church, and misery for all in the name of Christ. James II came to the throne in 1685—the Catholic king of a protestant country. In a bid to prevent discord in the state machinery, monarchs from Elizabeth I onwards had legislated against non-protestants holding public office. The logic was that you can only serve one master: so for an English protestant, the head of his church was also his monarch; but a Catholic had split loyalties, as the Pope was both head of his church and a head of state. The Pope's policy was usually in conflict with England's, so Catholics were seen as fifth columnists.

James II naturally tried to reverse this policy. He repealed anti-Catholic legislation, appointed Catholics to key public positions, and then legislated against protestants holding public office—and against them bearing arms.

A constitutional problem arose when protestants were separated from their arms: they were being denied their common-law right to defend themselves. Quite right too, James II would have said, as defending themselves would interfere with the way he wanted to run the country. In the run-up to the Glorious Revolution of 1688, Prince William of Orange was canvassed about his attitude to the common law. His response was to draft the of Declaration of Rights, indicating that he would sweep away any and all legislation—most of it generated by James II—that conflicted with the common law.

Once he was in England and crowned as King, William issued the Bill of Rights confirming that every citizen was entitled to all the privileges of his citizenship, regardless of religion. This, says the Bill of Rights, entitled protestants to get their arms out of the cupboard and wear them again, according to the law. It is important to recognize that the law the Bill of Rights speaks of here is the *common* law. There wasn't any other. One should note too that since the Declaration of Rights and the Bill of Rights are not Parliamentary legislation, Parliament can't amend or repeal them. The Bill of Rights merely reconfirms the common law, which Parliament didn't pass in the first place. A similar approach can be seen in the American constitution; it doesn't break new ground, it simply articulates and affirms what the common law already gave the people.

After the Bill of Rights was published, the English essentially had a constitution guaranteeing them all the rights, liberties and privileges of being English; we also have natural rights and God-given rights, which man cannot put asunder. Scottish rights are slightly different, since their legal base is a Roman system of codified law rather than a common law one. King Robert the Bruce had, in 1320 published the Declaration of Arbroath, which said that the people were sovereign;

this was because in his day one could not be king without the Pope's permission. The Bruce decided that, in Scotland at least, what the people thought mattered more than what the Pope thought.

In 1707, the Treaty of Union between England and Scotland gave the Scots all the rights and privileges of being British, being part of England. It also gave Englishmen Scottish rights. Devolution led to the Scotland Act, 1998, which upholds the European Convention on Human Rights (1966); the Scottish Parliament cannot pass legislation that would conflict with the Convention. The rest of the UK is covered by the Human Rights Act, 1998, which does the same thing: and the UK government cannot amend the European Convention on Human Rights, as they didn't pass it.

We have largely ignored the position in Ireland, because no constitutional implications for our history of firearms legislation arose there until the 20th century. We should note that the Gun Licensing Act of 1870 did not apply to Ireland, nor did the Pistols Act 1903. Likewise, the post-1968 firearms amendment Acts don't extend to Northern Ireland, so you can still go there to shoot pistols if you want. Otherwise, for the time being, we will simply note that the Bill of Rights is still in effect, because it can't be amended or re-pealed, in Great Britain and Northern Ireland.

Where the sun never set

The British took their system of common law with them as they sailed out to found their overseas empire. While their eastern colonial holdings were largely peaceful during the 18th century, the western arm in North America was anything but. The French nominally held a vast tract of land in what is now the southern and west United States (and was finally bought by the American colonists from a hard-up Napoleon in 1803), but exploited little of it; whereas French efforts to expand their northern territories outward from Quebec weren't finally quelled until 1759. Then the farmers and planters and intellectuals of the Thirteen Colonies to the south grew restive.

The founding fathers of those colonies had, generally speaking, been religious nonconformists, for whom the protestant reformation had not gone far enough. And they were correspondingly outspoken. In search of freedom to worship in their own way, they settled the northern end of the eastern American seaboard, around Boston.

Perhaps inevitably, their 'freedom' soon began to express itself in a form of authoritarian theocracy. Local governments handed down progressively harsher punishments for 'crimes' of non-compliance with their brand of religion. Eventually the Hanoverian King George

III intervened, following an appeal from a colonist, and prohibited the colonial administrations from enforcing non-conformist worship with painful penalties. During the 1760s the British Crown passed other legislation that affected colonists, who became increasingly incensed, as they had no moderating voice in Parliament. It is the phrase 'No taxation without representation' that is remembered today as the slogan of burgeoning insurrection.

The colonists had no army of their own but, as you'd expect, had a militia system: able-bodied men kept arms at home and could be turned out as a military force when there was a threat. Threats there were; the land had been wrested from native tribes in the first place. So, although the white settlers had the coast, inland there were still native Americans with attitude—and they were supported on occasion by Britain's other enemies, such as the French. The fragility of peace in the colonies was exposed when the British administration tried to make policing the colonists easier by impounding their militia weapons. That resulted in 'the shot that echoed round the world', and kicked off America's War of Independence.

The American colonies declared their independence as the United States of America in 1776; it took until 1783 to free themselves of British rule. More colonial militia formations fought for the Crown than against it. Ultimately, the rebels won because they had French support—the war had become an extension of the conflict between Britain and France that started in medieval times and rattled on until the final defeat of Napoleon in 1815.

Between 1787 and 1788, representatives of the States thrashed out a constitution for their new nation. This was extended in 1791 with 10 amendments—the 'Bill of Rights' that affirmed and confirmed the common-law rights of individual citizens, inherited from the mother country. The second amendment declared that "the right of the people to keep and bear arms shall not be infringed."

A potential ambiguity in the amendment's wording was finally resolved in 2008 by the US Supreme Court, which ruled that this was an *individual* right in common with all others in the Bill of Rights. The Court reached back through pre-independence English case law to the words of Alfred the Great in coming to its decision. So US law now conforms more closely to English common law and custom than the British government would like its own law to do. Which is ironic.

The 19th century saw British interests overseas expand—despite, or perhaps because of, the loss of the American colonies, but largely in the name of suppressing the slave trade, and mostly at gunpoint by people on the ground, supported by the Royal Navy afloat. Firearms also developed apace: a soldier of 1799 would have needed retraining to use the weapons of 1899. Much of that development can be narrowed down to a 13-year slot in the middle of the 19th century.

In 1851, the standard military long-arm was a smooth-bored musket, loaded from the muzzle. By 1864 and largely courtesy of American War Between The States, frontline troops had breech-loaded rifles, and artillery units had machine guns as well as cannon. There was a second spurt in new firearms technology at the end of the century inspired by the invention of smokeless powders. These products, chemically quite corrosive but less bulky and not as sooty as black powder, became a catalyst in the development of repeating and automatic mechanisms.

A licence to do what you've always done

In the UK in 1870, between these two innovations, the Home Office slipped a Gun Licence Act through Parliament. Renewable annually and costing 10 shillings, this licensed owners to take their firearms beyond the curtilage of their dwellings. It wasn't popular with farmers, who now had to pay the government a tax to rid their own fields of pests and vermin. Note, though, that this was a *licence*— it granted a specific permission—and not a system of registering guns or limiting who could own what. When registration was introduced with the Firearms Act 1920, the bureaucrats then (and perhaps since) may have been mindful of the common-law right—which needs no one's permission—to bear arms for self-defence; and so they named the owners' document a *certificate* rather than a licence. The tag has survived to this day, perhaps for that very reason.

In 1870 too, the Home Office speculated whether or not handguns should be banned. What was going on, that civil servants should be thinking along those lines?

We're not sure what they thought the problem was, but it may be relevant that London had started to replace parish night-watchmen and magistrates' runners with police officers in 1829. For constitutional reasons, policemen—government employees—could not be routinely armed, because that would make a standing army of them. This might be a touchy point when they had to maintain order at large public gatherings. But the constables of the Metropolitan police still had the constitutional right to keep and bear arms as individuals, and it had to be recognized that they could not lose any of their rights as citizens just because they worked for the government.

The solution was to acknowledge that their common law rights were paramount; and policemen who go armed on duty still do so on that basis. Before the point was settled, officers did undoubtedly encounter armed citizens going about unlawful business, and the need to find a way to control armed villains, who would confront unarmed constables, would have been taxing official minds. Actual encounters were, then as now, comparatively rare. And only a civil servant would imagine that a blanket ban might affect the proclivities of the criminally inclined.

Policing was a new trick in the 19th century. It put a constant uniformed presence on the streets. A constable was a man who could co-ordinate the 'hue and cry' when a malefactor was spotted in the act and chased; a man who could communicate with his colleagues using a whistle; a man who could secure a crime scene for other investigators to study. A good example of what London policing became over two generations can be found in the 'Jack the Ripper' case in 1888. Most of the crime scenes, apart from Mary Kelly's, which was indoors, were under the control of a police officer within a matter of minutes after the murder.

Firearms feature not in the Ripper story. Although night-patrol officers were entitled to carry revolvers if they wished, and probably did, they had no occasion to use them in the course of the Ripper enquiry. The revolvers available for issue were cartridge models, although the transition from 'loose ammunition' cap-and-ball pistols was far from complete. The murdered girls themselves could have been armed, according to law, but weren't—for the simple reason that at their rates of pay they simply couldn't afford to buy the guns with which they might have defended themselves.

Home Office worries about handguns seem to have kicked off again near the end of the 19th century, when smokeless powders had enabled inventors to produce really small repeating pistols. The handgun market by the end of the 19th century consisted of pocket guns at one end of the scale—.25 automatics and .320 revolvers— and .455 revolvers and their equivalents from foreign manufacturers at the other end of the scale. The gap between was gradually filled by the likes of John Moses Browning and Smith & Wesson, with .38 taking centre ground. In Germany, Georg Luger adopted this calibre in a rimless cased cartridge for his refinement of Borchardt's automatic pistol design and, being foreign, he used the metric '9mm' for its diameter.

CHAPTER THREE

FIRST SQUEEZES OF THE LEMON

B RITAIN WAS AT WAR in South Africa when the country cele-
brated the arrival of the 20th century; the second Boer War
was the proving ground for the British Army's repeating rifles
and carbines, adopted in 1889 and upgraded several times thereafter.
When peace came, a War Office committee decided that the lessons
learned in the war pointed to issuing one type of rifle to all branches
of the military. Thus, the short, magazine, Lee Enfield (SMLE or
'Smelly') was born in 1903, and got its bridge guide for charger-clip
loading five years later.

The Home Office reacted by producing what became the Pistols
Act, 1903. This required that, if you wanted to purchase a firearm
with a barrel less than 9 inches long, you had to be 18 years old, and
either have a gun or game licence, or be a householder (that is, you
paid local property taxes). Retailers had to keep a register of all pistols
sold, and could be fined if they sold one to anyone who was drunk at
the time or, presumably manifestly, of unsound mind. The Act is
now remembered for only two things. One is *Gamage Ltd v. Bryson*
(1907), in which the police prosecuted the department store for selling air guns with less than 9 inches of pipe. The other is a gunmakers'
ruse: Webley and Hammerli, and perhaps others, produced single-
shot, 10-inch barrel pistols, which became the entry-level gun for
several generations of pistol shooters. A Great War committee
bitched that these long-barrelled pistols 'circumvented' the controls,
thereby showing that they failed to understand a simple principle—
that if you give maximum and minimum measurements in legislation,
that's what the trade will comply with. It's senseless to complain of
the obvious consequences of the clear wording of an Act.

As an illustration of the fatuousness of this kind of legislation,
consider shotgun barrel lengths. The shortest made are around 6
inches long, and the longest around 100 inches. The function of a

barrel's length is to burn all the powder provided to propel the shot, accelerating it up the barrel. The powder should be consumed as the shot reaches fresh air. If it isn't, you get a muzzle flash from powder burning after the shot has left the barrel. Obviously, shotgun cartridges can be loaded to match a given barrel length, so when Greener made 'pigeon guns' with 14-inch barrels, he also made compatible cartridges. Long barrels need slower burning magnum powders and so on: a balance has to be struck between the burn rate of the powder and the length of the barrel it gets to burn in. If you legislate for barrel length, guns will be made to comply and ammunition will be reconfigured to be most efficient. Barrel length *per se* doesn't have much to do with the lethality of a shotgun, although it does influence its effective range.

British legislation on shotguns has specified various measurements over time; first, in 1937, was the 20-inch minimum barrel length for shotguns. This was extended in 1965 to 24 inches. Then in 1988 came the equally arbitrary minimum *overall* length of 40 inches for repeating shotguns. These magic numbers, we are told, contribute to maintaining public safety and the Queen's peace.

Nothing like a drama to make a knee jerk

Back in the Edwardian era, concern in government circles about the private possession of firearms was fanned by the occasional dramatic incident. In particular there were the 'Tottenham Outrage' of 1909 (a failed armed robbery and a subsequent hue and cry after the suspects, during which over a thousand rounds were fired), and the 'siege of Sydney Street' in 1910, when foreign anarchists were besieged and then burned out of a house in east London, having first drawn attention to themselves by shooting at various people, including a number of police officers.

There would have been a gun-control bill in 1911, but for lack of Parliamentary time. The Edwardian government was upset because of occasional brawls and street fights involving guns, and shots had sometimes been fired at police; six constables were shot dead in the five years 1908–12. This was uncivilized behaviour, rather than organized crime. It was an interesting year, 1911, anyway. Lack of Parliamentary time was due to some extent to the need to pass more pressing legislation—the Parliament Act and the Official Secrets Act, for instance, not to mention some disruption as the crown passed to King George V. Then the clouds of war gathered; and in 1917 Sir Ernley Blackwell was instructed to form a committee to consider the position *à propos* firearms when peace replaced war. His report was provided to Christopher Addison, the Minister for Reconstruction, just four days after the armistice in 1918.

All those on the committee seem to have been civil servants and thus, it seems, of similar mind-set. None had any legal training. They had two things to worry about—how to dispose of stocks of military weapons after the war, and what to do about the large number of well-trained ex-servicemen returning to civilian life. Disposing of firearms was seen as a problem in the domestic market and in the tribal areas on the edges of empire, by which they meant Afghanistan in particular. Since the Afghan tribes already suffered no lack of rifles, the trick was to cut off their supplies of ammunition. The committee, perhaps not surprisingly for men of their station, was more preoccupied by the prospect of disaffected returning servicemen joining forces with the working class and what they (had they read too much Joseph Conrad?) called "the anarchist or 'intellectual' malcontent of the great cities, whose weapons are the bomb and the automatic pistol" to replicate Russia's Bolshevik revolution in England.

Blackwell's report is an entirely bureaucratic solution to a non-existent problem. He proposed licensing the gun trade and individual owners, as well as imports and exports of arms, and using all said licenses as ways to restrict possession. Into the bargain, he proposed considerable government discretion as to who could get what. His default position was that "the control of firearms should be made far more stringent than it is now is a proposition which hardly anyone could be found to question", which was itself questionable. There was no original thinking in his report and no real evidence to support his conclusions. Most of the domestic issues were considered in the context of information gathered in the run-up to the—subsequently abandoned—1911 bill. Any evidence Blackwell collected during the war was simply from other civil servants, as to how the bureaucracy would work. Nobody considered that people might choose not to comply with any new law, or what to do if existing firearms owners chose to ignore an edict whose advantage they failed to perceive.

The place is teeming with guns. Pass the ammunition

The problem as far as the domestic market was concerned was that the horse had already bolted. Servicemen had been bringing guns back as souvenirs that they'd captured, liberated, stolen, bartered or won in card games ever since British forces went abroad to execute British government foreign policy. The government itself had been giving away captured German rifles, machine guns and field artillery to buyers of war bonds. Even as Blackwell handed in his report to

Addison, British troops were searching abandoned German positions for souvenirs.

Not that Britain was exactly firearms-poor before the war. Before the formation of the territorial army in 1908, members of volunteer rifle regiments had purchased their own rifles, as they had been doing collectively in clubs or volunteer regiments since 1860. Belgian imports from 1904 to 1914 amounted to over 4 million guns of all types. The FN Model 1889 was the first repeating service rifle available on the open market in that late 19th-century spurt of development, and they proved popular with rifle clubs and volunteer units until Lee Enfield production satisfied military demand and the trade could get the parts to make them.

There were many revolvers, of course. Belgian companies made lots of versions for pinfire ammunition, and cap-and-ball was still popular. Many of Browning's early pistol designs were launched from Belgium. Belgian production was destroyed by the war: its centre was Liège, which was reduced to rubble in the autumn of 1914. Belgium was only one of a number of countries from which firearms were imported into the UK; popular Edwardian pocket pistols included French, German and American models.

The birth of bureaucratic rule

Blackwell's recommendations became the basis of the Firearms Act, 1920, the bulk of which reads as quite modern—because it has been carried forward and added to since. The Act made it unlawful for anyone to "purchase, have in his possession, use, or carry any firearm or ammunition unless he holds a certificate (in this Act called a firearm certificate) granted under this section, and in force at the time." The certificate, valid for three years, "shall be granted by the chief officer of police of the district in which the applicant for the certificate resides, if he is satisfied that the applicant is a person who has a good reason for requiring such a certificate and can be permitted to have in his possession, use, and carry a firearm or ammunition without danger to the public safety or to the peace, and on payment of the prescribed fee." Debate in Parliament had already established that "good reason" would include keeping a pistol to defend house, home, and family. It may all have seemed harmless enough, but it turned out to be the thin end of a very fat wedge.

The bureaucrats seem to have underestimated the paperwork the Act would generate, much as Beveridge did a generation later—when he calculated the costs of a national health service, he assumed the costs of dental treatment and glasses were one-off: he didn't allow for repeat treatments. Blackwell's thinking was similarly two-dimensional. He assumed that those entitled to certificates would get them; his report is silent about the position of those not eligible for certificates—and there's no suggestion that there should be an amnesty or (mercifully) a national search of property.

The real problem, that millions of trained men would be returning to a land where there were no jobs, was not addressed by Blackwell. To be fair to the government of the day, they were much closer to surrounding events than we are, and they had experienced first-hand revolution in Ireland and Mexico; they'd seen the Imperial Russian government dissolve into the Soviet revolution, and subsequent civil war there. Four empires collapsed as the Great War ended, meaning a change of government for many countries in Europe, Africa and the Middle East. Civil war raged in Ireland after partition; there seemed to be instability everywhere. It must have been a frightening time to be holed up in an ivory tower.

The problem with not terribly good law

To call the 1920 Firearms Act a mistake is to oversimplify matters. The Britain of 1919 was well stocked with weapons of all sizes, most of them under government control, and most of those were rapidly becoming redundant. Weapons are an asset until the problem they were created (or acquired) to deal with is resolved. Then they become a liability. The bigger the stuff, the bigger the liability—take battleships then, for example, or nuclear weapons today. Lorries, motorbikes and aircraft did hit the post-war civilian market, as you'd expect. The rifles went into store, to reappear in 1939.

That was also true of the civilian market. Most people who had firearms kept them because they appeared to be an asset. Once the perceived need for them diminished, they became something of a liability. Sitting in a drawer or cupboard, harmless enough, millions of guns sat unused, awaiting developments. A few hardy souls obtained the new certificates for their firearms, but there lay the problem. The legislation created a pool of unregistered stuff, officially making criminals of numerous war heroes and their families, as well as warbond investors and anyone else who had a gun but for one reason or another didn't get around to registering it.

Once the Act settled down, it was obvious that the vast majority of gun owners had ignored it. The number of firearms on certificate was less than a tiny fraction of even the most pessimistic estimates of the numbers of firearms in the UK. There were two issues, really. The requirement to hold a certificate means doing something to get it; and *not* doing so muddles the other issue—what to do about people who, in the government's mind, shouldn't have one anyway. We will return to this point later, as it features heavily in the current debate as to where any such bar should be set.

In principle, we are all equal before the law, so setting a bar at all means making an arbitrary decision. The 1903 Act limited retail sales to people over 18 who had a gun licence (bought at the Post Office), or who were householders intending to keep their pistol at home. Simple enough, but still clearly a bar: one that's partly financial, but also partly to do with status, also known as apparent respectability.

Firearms law was next reviewed in 1934 by the Bodkin Committee. They collected data about the misuse of guns that weren't regulated by the 1920 Act, shot pistols in particular. In the end the recommendations they made for further legislation seem to have been based on the Federal law passed in the US in 1934. The most obvious example of a transatlantic influence is the view they took of fully automatic firearms. Not one instance of misuse, or use in crime in the UK, was detected by the committee, but they recommended banning them anyway. Such weapons had no advocates. According to legend, their main detractors were the British Deer Society, who merely stated the obvious and declared machine guns unsuitable for stalking. Existing owners just kept quiet, while those who had registered their weapons were rewarded with the additional authority they needed to keep them, until a new policy was promulgated in 1973.

The Bodkin committee did not consider whether the registration system set up by the 1920 Act was worthwhile or not. That wasn't in their remit; in much the same way, the Home Affairs Committee didn't ask the right questions in 2010. It's easier to rub along making things worse than it is to sort them out. After all, making the problem worse—more complicated—is one way to guarantee a bureaucrat's or a policeman's continued employment. Bodkin's recommendations became the 1936 (Amendment) Act followed by a 1937 Act of consolidation. The only real attempt at doing anything about the pool of unregistered firearms was various amnesties, in which the public were invited to give away property they'd bought, earned, inherited or won, with no discernible benefit either to themselves or (for those who cared to think about it) to their government.

A very great war indeed

The Second World War didn't sneak up on the British public in the way the Great War had: nobody believed in Chamberlain's 'peace in our time' and, to be fair, Chamberlain didn't believe in it himself.

The government used the time he'd bought with his 'piece of paper' brought home from Munich to get ready for what was coming. In the year of grace from 1938 to 1939, they completed the chain home radar stations, recruited the Observer Corps, started national conscription and issued gas masks to everyone. The first eight-gun monoplane Hawker Hurricane fighter aircraft started to reach front line squadrons, soon followed by the Supermarine Spitfire. Mechanization of the army was completed in 1939, when the last cavalry units received armoured vehicles. The government also ordered a million cardboard coffins.

There must, in 1940, have been a considerable body of opinion, among senior bureaucrats and the more visible members of the ruling élite in the UK, to the effect that the war would end with German forces occupying the French channel ports: that an armistice with Germany, or some treaty, would conclude hostilities and that Hitler wouldn't invade Britain. There were similar thoughts in Germany, as Hitler spent June dithering about what to do as well.

Once Churchill became prime minster in May 1940, it was obvious that no such bargain was in the offing: keeping the war going was the only option for both sides. That's when the rifles came out of store; a lot of local defence volunteers had put weapons down against future needs and got them out again. Six weeks later, when the government sent out the codeword CROMWELL, for 'invasion imminent', a million men had joined the Home Guard. It's easy to underestimate this body of men if you've only seen *Dad's Army* re-runs on TV. But don't. In 1914, the equivalent home defence force in Liège, armed only with rifles, derailed the entire German strategy for winning that war by Christmas. Chances are, our militia would have done at least as well, or died trying.

Civilian firearm certificates necessarily took a back seat during the war. Huge numbers of rifles that had been privately preserved saw action for the second time, while young men joining the commandos went scrounging for the heavier revolvers of the previous generation. Much of the Home Guard's early weaponry came out of places it had been hidden by people who didn't trust their government enough to hand it in when they were supposed to. Government stores were soon opened and kit dished out, but the Home Guard was always kept short of ammunition. One of our informants was in the Polish army prior to 1988, and he said they had the same problem: most of the ammunition was kept in Russia. If the West invaded, the Poles would be retreating towards their ammunition; meanwhile, they never had enough in Poland to mount an invasion of Russia. The paranoid shade of Sir Ernley Blackwell still stalked the corridors of power in 1940, and damn the consequences if the Germans did invade.

The Home Guard's actual work involved guarding the coast and locating downed fliers and their machines, and manning anti-aircraft and searchlight batteries—they were involved in every aspect of war on the Home Front. They were a classic militia in the sense that Alfred the Great intended. It's interesting that they were disbanded in 1944, just after D-Day, when the outcome of the invasion was far from certain. V-weapons were falling on the southeast daily and the reversals of Arnhem and the Bulge hadn't happened when they were demobilized. Was that a question of costs, or of civil service nervousness about the public being armed and keeping weapons at home?

The pool of unregistered weapons gets deeper yet

On demobilization, a vast amount of the Home Guards' kit, some of it issue kit, went back into cupboards. Whatever hand-in arrangements were made in 1944 were far from comprehensive, or perhaps we should say effective. After a pint or two, Colin Greenwood will tell of a lady handing in the Home Guard Bren gun in the 1968 amnesty. We met one chap at Bisley in the 1980s who was using up Home Guard ammunition—and replacing it in the stockpile with new stuff. We also know of a highly respectable businessman, since deceased, who kept a Colt .45 M1911A acquired in Burma until the early 1970s. And so it goes on.

The current Home Office guidance to the police says that firearms issued to or captured by Britain's armed forces since 1939 are government property; what we don't know is when they decided that. As indicated, we know returning servicemen in the 1940s brought back souvenirs with them, and there were other sources as well. Here are a few more anecdotes. Names have been changed to protect the guilty.

Harry was a prisoner of war in Changhi camp, Singapore, from 1942 until '45. When Japan surrendered, Allied forces moved quickly to secure a supply route to the camp. Harry emerged from captivity with the Webley revolver he'd hidden at the time of surrender, and a Japanese pistol he'd stolen during captivity. He brought them back as souvenirs, eventually dumping them during a house-move clearout.

Nicolas joined the RAF and served in the UK guarding German PoWs, one of whom swapped him a .32 pistol for a bar of chocolate. He carried the pistol while stationed in Germany doing the same sort of work and let it go in one of the later amnesties. Nigel did likewise: he'd kept his Dad's Colt New Service, which had seen action in the Great War, for his own use when he was a commando in the Second

World War. He sold it, and a captured Walther PP, in the early 1990s, as part of his clearout prior to moving into an old peoples' home.

In the 1980s, Matthew bought a Colt Series 80 .45 semi-auto pistol to continue his club training. He showed it to his Mum, who said it was very nice, just like her one. "Her what?" It turned out that she'd dated a trooper of an American airborne division, and in 1944 he'd given her a mint M1911A1, promising he'd be back for it and for her. He didn't return, so 40 years later she still had the piece in her bedside table drawer.

Even little old ladies do it: let's do it

An old lady brought her late husband's cache to our offices during the 1988 amnesty: a Mauser broomhandle, an M1911A1 and a Smith & Wesson Victory, all won in a single poker game in Berlin in 1945.

Geoff joined the RAF Regiment in 1945 and in his first action—defending RAF property from feral gangs of ex-German soldiers—he shot a guy with his Enfield revolver. The bullet didn't penetrate, but knocked him over. He surrendered, handing Geoff a 9mm Browning GP35A, made by the Belgian factory during the German occupation. Geoff kept it until he left the RAF in the 1970s, after which it enjoyed a second career in service pistol competitions, then in practical pistol and finally—well, never mind.

Some people kept their souvenirs, others didn't. Alex accepted an M1934 Beretta pistol from an Italian submarine officer (he was on a destroyer and the Italian submarine was floating around looking for someone to surrender to). By the end of the war he'd used up 12 of the 16 cartridges it came with, so he dropped it in Dover harbour on his return for demobilization.

Despite all this weaponry floating around, and despite the best efforts of the media (such as the film The Blue Lamp in 1949), firearms crime in the UK remained stubbornly low after the war. The 1920 Act had come in on the back of an average of four armed robberies a year, and a handful of other incidents in which shots were fired. Government concern in 1917 focussed on 'intellectual malcontents' whose weapons were allegedly the pistol and the bomb. Anarchists and revolutionaries have used the latter to devastating effect far more often, but the powers-that-be still obsess about handguns. 'Intellectual malcontents' have now been rebranded as 'terrorists', but they still prefer explosives to firearms in pursuit of their strange, self-defeating agendas.

People who kept firearms on certificate were few in number in the 1950s and mostly middle class. The top drawer, if Lord Montgomery and Sir Winston Churchill are anything to go by, never troubled with certificates at all. Neither did the subculture that kept them for emergencies or as tools of their trade.

Rights, duties, obligations—and taxes

So far, we haven't dwelt much on the constitutional position, so a little widening of perspective is called for. The right to defend one-self, to preserve your liberty and that of others, and to protect your friends, family and property, is a common-law right. This isn't a matter of vigilante action or 'taking the law into your own hands'. The law is *already* in your hands, whether you like it or not. Think of it as a policing duty; you are the line the bad guy has to cross to steal from you or to harm your family. You have a clear duty to stop him from doing so, but the only penalty if you do nothing is that he gets away with it. He punishes you by taking your property, stealing your sheep, violating your daughter. Of course, you might be able to get back at him later through the justice system, but that doesn't neces-sarily restore the *status quo ante*. Any sweets he took will have been eaten, and anyone he killed is still dead.

The obligation to turn out for your government as a militia in an emergency is still a common-law obligation. Last invoked in Britain in 1940, it's largely been superseded by maintaining what is a *de facto* standing ('regular') army and a territorial reserve. In effect, you have delegated those people to defend the realm on your behalf, and they are paid to do so from the taxes you shell out to the government.

This is also true of policing. Your taxes pay some people to serve you in the office of constable to uphold the law on behalf of us all. The difference between you and a policeman is that you have the option of doing nothing about a crime being committed against you; he is paid to deal with it, so it's his obligation and he has no dis-cretion to avoid that duty. That you're paying him to do it doesn't mean you aren't allowed to intervene. You still can, and anyway you may be first one to the crime scene. You might *be* the crime scene. What you should do is hand over control of the scene to the first uniformed public servant to arrive.

Defence of the realm is a trickier question. While the individual right or duty seems to be limited to being appropriately prepared, it's the government who mobilizes the militia. Without that mobilization, individuals who resist an enemy of the realm are acting solely in defence of their own lives, liberty and property, as civilians. The call-out makes you a member of the militia, with wider powers of inter-vention, as when Alfred the Great wanted you somewhere, or when

Churchill did a thousand years later. The callout also changes your status from civilian to military, thus giving you recognition as a soldier under various conventions. As a soldier, you can take offensive action against your realm's enemies; as a civilian, common law limits you to defensive action. The question is whether government provision of an army and a police force in any way limits your rights as an individual.

The answer seems to be No, if the US Supreme Court interpreted British law correctly when considering the second amendment in 2008. There is obviously less likelihood of your being called out to serve as militia these days, but it happened in 1940 because the government had no other way on hand to deal with the sudden threat of invasion. The key difference between then (and now) and the original concept of the militia is that Alfred the Great and most of his successors made no financial provision for equipping a militia, whereas modern governments have collected revenue to do so.

Our summary is: that in time of national peril your individual rights are unimpaired, but the chances of having to reciprocate those rights by fulfilling your obligation to turn out for your government are much reduced by your tax burden. So, if you're entitled to defend yourself and you are entitled to have the means to do so, what's the point of a firearm certificate system that tries to prevent you?

Policy changes practice, but doesn't change the law

The 1920 Act was a panic measure, fuelled by a fear of imminent socialist insurrection. It was also directed solely at firearms kept for sporting purposes and not those held for defence. By the time of the next review of the law, the Act had its feet under the table. It didn't catch occupational users who benefitted from the common law, so nobody was rubbing up against its restrictions, as it did not claim any impact on common law rights. By the time the legislation was reconsidered in the 1930s, there didn't seem to be any pressing reason to change things, and the committee wasn't mandated to deliberate on that question anyway.

There was a subtle change after the Second World War, which was a gradual take-up of certificates by people who hadn't troubled in 1920. Given that guns kept for lawful purposes other than sporting use didn't need certificates, a small problem arose when people wanted to buy ammunition. The trouble with such an exemption is that you haven't got anything to prove it applies to you. The solution was to get a firearm certificate for convenience, to simplify the business of buying replacement ammunition.

This practice continued into the 1950s, when government policy quietly changed. They made a unilateral decision around the time of the Prevention of Crime Act 1953—which introduced the concept of an 'offensive weapon'—that wanting to keep firearms for self-defence would no longer be a 'good reason' to issue certificates for those weapons. This change of policy *should* have caused no difficulty, of course, as those firearms needn't and shouldn't have been on certificate in the first place. The change, which has never had the force of law, merely reversed a bureaucratic simplification of the ammunition supply chain. The trouble is, that's not what the civil servants meant. They weren't reverting some certificate holders to an exemption: they were trying to remove guns from those people altogether.

When the man in Whitehall knows best...

The public face of this policy was presented in the form of un-helpful advice: that (a) if you don't resist, your attacker is less likely to harm you and (b) if you do have a weapon, your attacker is likely to take it off you and harm you with it.

That's really sloppy thinking. If you are attacked by a hungry bear, behaving like a cheeseburger only compounds the problem. Violent attackers use intimidation to get what they want in the first place, but quite often use violence afterwards to make their getaway more certain. You can't chase someone if you're unconscious, or preoccupied with your newly-acquired broken jaw.

The second point is born of plain stupidity, but it does highlight another issue. Yes, if you have a weapon and no training in how to use it, there might be a way for an attacker to take it off you. Training is the key. A trained man can show a potential aggressor that he's armed and ready. Showing your awareness of the threat is the battle half-won. It discourages the would-be attacker and means that no crime takes place.

Bureaucrats and police sometimes refer to this as displacement—meaning that you've shifted the crime from being an attack on you, to becoming an attack on someone else. That's a lazy argument. In showing the street thug what might happen to him if he doesn't behave, we've prevented one or more crimes and re-educated the thug. The bureaucrat is assuming he'll get over the shock of that encounter with us quickly enough to want to have a go at someone else almost immediately. The bureaucrat is also assuming that the next person along won't be armed.

Displacement works as an argument some of the time; if a burglar is desperate to burgle somewhere, the shuttered and alarmed house will be crossed off his list first. His problem is that the houses that remain accessible may have little of value in them and may not be worth the risk. Government policy has put much emphasis on passive security. Today's cars are much harder to steal than those made in 1980, and houses are harder to get into. The weak point in both instances is the same—the keyholder. So now, being prepared and having the means to face down a villain in person is more necessary than ever.

The change in public policy actually made little difference. The kind of crimes one might prevent by being armed were rare before 1954 and remained rare after 1954. What the change did was to give the powers-that-be an excuse to prosecute people who armed themselves on the off-chance of being attacked. The move was largely directed at the youth gangs of the period, although subsequent policing seems to have been directed at everybody but. Those who had firearms for defence on certificates either took them off and reverted to their position under the common law, or kept them on with a change of use, such as 'pest control'.

PART TWO

WHEN IN DOUBT, BAN IT

It is the invariable habit of bureaucracies, at all times and everywhere, to assume... that every citizen is a criminal. Their one apparent purpose, pursued with a relentless and furious diligence, is to convert the assumption into a fact. They hunt endlessly for proofs, and, when proofs are lacking, for mere suspicions. The moment they become aware of a definite citizen, John Doe, seeking what is his right under the law, they begin searching feverishly for an excuse for withholding it from him.
—H.L. Mencken

If we can ever make red tape nutritional, we can feed the world.
—Robert Schaeberle

I am convinced that we can do to guns what we've done to drugs: create a multi-billion dollar underground market over which we have absolutely no control.
—George L. Roman

CHAPTER FOUR

INTO THE SWINGING SIXTIES

L ABOUR WON the general election in 1964 by a whisker. Among
its policy objectives was abolishing the death penalty. This was
still a sentencing option for a few crimes and was last carried
out early in 1964, when two men were executed for murder in the
course of a robbery. Other capital crimes included murder with firearms or explosives, murder of a police or prison officer, and a second
murder by any means. The Labour government achieved a five-year
'experimental' suspension (an unfortunate choice of word) of capital
punishment, with the result that in 1966 a succession of nasty people
who would otherwise have been hanged became famous instead. Not
everyone swung in the Sixties who might have.

The 'moors murderers' Myra Hindley and Ian Brady would have
been dropped, having been convicted of more than one murder each.
The Kray twins Ronnie and Reggie would have qualified for the same
reason. One of their murders, of George Cornell, was committed
with a firearm, and their second murder, of Jack McVitie, would have
been too, if the gun had worked. Harry Roberts really racked up the
debate when he and accomplices used handguns to shoot dead three
London policemen on 12 August 1966. Calls to restore the death
penalty were loud and persistent. Home Secretary Roy Jenkins sought
to divert attention from that by cracking down on firearms.

A private member's bill in 1965 had extended the minimum barrel
length for a shotgun from 20 inches to 24. The main victims of this
alteration were owners of American guns; repeaters tended to be
made with 20-inch barrels to keep the overall length down, as they
have longer receivers than break-action singles and doubles. Some
owners put their guns onto firearm certificates and a few had a barrel
extension fitted, but most didn't hear of the change until years later.

An internal Home Office review in 1965 had considered introducing a certificate system for shotguns and had concluded that the

costs of administration outweighed any benefit. Shotgunners already had to buy a Post Office licence for each gun until this was abolished by the Local Government Act in 1966, so they were, in effect, registering the existence of their guns and paying 10 shillings a year for each one. Harry Roberts, of course, wasn't into Post Office gun licences and had used handguns for the murders. Shotguns didn't feature in any of the crimes drawn into the debate on capital punishment and only rarely featured in the statistics at all, but Roy Jenkins needed a scapegoat. He chose to introduce shotgun certificates.

The requirement to hold such a certificate appeared as an amendment to the Criminal Justice Bill 1967, after which an act of consolidation in 1968 drew the legislation together, carrying forward the provisions for firearm certificates in the 1920 Act and those of the 1937 Act. The 1968 Act's section 1 covers firearms; section 2 deals with shotguns; and section 5 covers machine guns and other 'prohibited' weapons. The immediate impact of the 1967 and '68 Acts was that only a small proportion of shotgun owners applied for the new certificates. There were about 600,000 applications in the first year, which represented about 10 percent of shotgun owners and users.

The Home Office prepared a memorandum to police and issued it to chief constables for the guidance of those in his employ who had to issue certificates. This document, in 1969, was 'restricted' to your servants in the police. You couldn't buy it, as the Home Office saw fit never to publish it. The impact of the guidance was a steady increase in the use of conditions on firearm certificates. Before 1969, conditions were exceptional. After 1969, they became standard, such as the one decreeing that firearms held for target shooting could be used only on ranges with an MoD safety certificate. This had to be dumped in 2006, when the MoD stopped checking ranges.

The secret machinations of the mysterious John McKay

The next turn of events was, again in secret, the appointment in the early Seventies of John McKay (later knighted) to review firearms legislation. As with previous committees convened to discuss the subject, all the people around McKay's table were civil servants without legal training. His committee took no independent evidence, although a sub-committee met with various interest groups, including the national shooting organizations, the gun trade, the National Farmers Union and the British Deer Society. McKay's background was in policing. Submitted in September 1972, his report has never been published, although a Home Officer minister was persuaded to put a copy in the House of Commons library 25 years later. We had our copy from someone who managed to get his *via* the US Freedom of Information Act.

By that time we all knew much of what was in it, because the Home Secretary who received it used it as the basis for a Green Paper published in 1973 (Cmnd 5297) as a consultation document. That was the first time, as far as we know, that there was any public consultation about firearms law, and the public swiftly condemned the whole package.

The shooting organizations* had, until that point, never been a gun lobby. All of them had been formed as governing bodies for various aspects of the shooting sports in the days before the Competition Act. But the Green Paper brought them all together in opposition to government for the first time, in the shape of the Longroom Committee, so-named after the boardroom they met in at Purdey's; this became the British Shooting Sports Council in the 1970s.

So what was it in the 1973 Green Paper that united all gun users against the government's proposals? It called for a ban on self-loading rifles, pump action and semi-automatic shotguns—all of them 19th-century technology. An end to the separate category for shotguns and their certificates—which had been introduced (controversially) only five years earlier, and with no evidence that the legislation in force was a failure (or indeed worth keeping). They also proposed to remove all firearms taking metal cartridges from antique status,

---

* The oldest of these was the National Rifle Association. Essentially a side-branch of the volunteer rifle regiment movement and founded in 1860, its original function was to organize competitions for riflemen on Wimbledon Common. They moved to Bisley Camp, near Brookwood in Surrey, in the 1890s, and various rifle clubs joined them there, building pavilions and catering facilities for their members. Rifle and pistol shooting as a sport and the volunteer rifle regiments diverged as the 19th century progressed. Some people were in the regiments as militia, ready to be called out when needed; others were in it for the social life; while some regiments gradually went on to specialize in sports other than shooting.

Some volunteer rifle regiments saw action in the Boer War, which exposed the shortcomings of that system and resulted in the government forming the territorial reserve in 1908. The NRA continued as a sporting competition organizer, and made a further departure from the military in 1957: when the army adopted a semi-automatic rifle, the NRA decided to stay with bolt-action target rifles. They did maintain the service rifle events, but it would be 25 years before a civilian shot service rifle at Bisley again.

The National Smallbore Rifle Association developed from earlier organizations such as the Working Men's Rifle Association, and governed .22 shooting. On the shotgun side, the Wildfowlers Association of Great Britain and Northern Ireland and the Clay Pigeon Shooting Association represented live quarry and artificial target shooting respectively. Trade associations existed for gun dealers, gamekeepers *et al.*

ignoring the fact that this would include weapons made in the early 19th century and already well over a century old at the time they were writing. The paper proposed an end to collecting as a good reason, and thought that keeping family heirlooms should not be acceptable as a reason for families to hold on to firearms they already owned— for many generations in some cases. Many proposals would have made the police far more central to the-day-to-day running of fire-arms dealerships, i.e. had them snooping into transactions between people already considered fit to have firearms. In sum, the Green Paper was proposing a hugely increased bureaucracy without any benefit to public safety for the costs generated. It reeked of more regulation, for regulation's sake.

When politicians fail, send in the police

The excuse on offer for making these significant changes was the usual suspect: an allegedly increasing use of guns in crime. Never mind that much of the 'increase' was generated by manipulation of statistics. The rest of it was down to a combination of the inability of the police to perform their duty to maintain public safety effectively, and new crimes created by recent legislation. The main 'increase' was admitted to be in air-gun crime, but that was a product of the way in which the data were collected. Criminal damage using an air gun was recorded if the cost of the damage exceeded £20. Between 1967 and '71, more crimes entered the figures because inflation meant that £20 bought less and less replacement glass. Air guns were also admitted to be the main cause of most 'firearms' injuries. On the back of what kids chose to do when they lacked adequate facilities for shooting air guns safely, the government was proposing massive changes to the landscape in which adults used real firearms responsibly, and had done so for decades on end.

The Tory government of 1973 had no particular axe to grind over firearms, so saw no problem in going public with the Green Paper. In any event they had other problems to deal with, not least of which was a national strike by mineworkers. This led to a partial shutdown of British industry and eventually to a general election. The Green Paper died with the old government. Civil servants, however, did not forget it—they never do: they simply bided their time.

While the new Labour government made no fresh moves to re-strict the public's access to shooting, chief constables did. Some re-commendations in the McKay report became police policy, such as the one that suggested that collecting should no longer be a good reason for owning firearms. At much the same time, the Home

Office took over responsibility for issuing section 5 (prohibited weapons) authorities from the Defence Council, and with the change of management came a change of policy. Machine-gun collections were out, and section 5 was basically limited to people in the gun trade who imported and exported automatic weapons.

Apart from machine-gun collectors, however, few people were directly affected. Although most military rifles (but not the British L1A1) were selective, changing to full-auto and semi-auto fire at the flick of a switch, those who made such rifles made semi-auto-only variants for the civilian market. The Seventies were years of increasing prosperity for many people—incomes rose, giving a lot of working-class people greater disposable wealth—and that is reflected in the increased take-up of shotgun certificates at this time.

New shooters are born, old ones emerge from the woodwork

Two things were going on, we think. Obviously, increased prosperity meant that more people took up activities such as clay pigeon shooting; and pistol shooting, hitherto a small clique appended to rifle clubs, also took off. The reason for the latter has to do with real estate. A pistol range makes a comparatively small footprint; you can fit one into an industrial unit, or a redundant quarry, or a corner of the rifle range, whereas fullbore rifle ranges can take up golf course-sized pieces of land. For clay-pigeon shooting, all that's needed is space for the shot to fall in and an area for the launching traps.

The growth in pistol shooting is not well-reflected in the firearm certificate figures. That may be because the police were actively shaking out of the system the inactive certificate holders—it got harder to renew a certificate if you weren't using your rifles. And, of course, existing certificate holders who added pistols to their rifle certificates would not increase the number of certificate holders.

The increased availability of facilities, in the form of *ad-hoc* clubs meeting in fields, meant that a lot of shotgun owners belatedly bowed to the law and acquired certificates. It wasn't much of a problem, as until 1989 there was no obligation to list one's guns on an application form or the ticket itself or to explain where they came from. From 1968 until 1989, the shotgun certificate was essentially a fit-person certificate. It authorized the holder to possess shotguns in much the same way that a TV licence authorizes the use of any number of (unregistered) televisions at the licensed address.

An incident in 1981 when blank shots were fired near HM the Queen during the ceremony of Trooping the Colour led to a short Firearms Act, which paved the way to guidance to the trade as to how to manufacture (or adapt) imitation firearms so that they were not 'readily convertible' to fire live ammunition. There had been a number of reproduction firearms imported—notably Spanish-made flintlocks and such—that could be made to fire simply by drilling the touch-hole through into the barrel. The guidance was quite comprehensive and paved the way to the trade deactivating real guns and selling them in the same way as they sold replicas.

Whim and caprice: police invent the laws they like

A decade after McKay's report, the shooter's landscape had changed quite a bit. Commercial interests meant that the trade had expanded, more firearms types were available through importers, and there were more ranges, more shooting clubs, and more organizations looking after them. A lot of Second World War kit, which had been kept in reserve in various places around the world, had started to move into the surplus market. The countries holding it had re-equipped—either with subsidized American rifles, surplus to US needs post-Vietnam, or with no-less-subsidized Kalashnikov rifles sold by the Soviet Union and China. These older firearms turned up on firearm certificates, modified to single shot where necessary, or smoothbored for shotgun certificate holders to collect, or deactivated as wall hangers.

The health of the shooting sports generally reflected the wealth and well-being of the country as a whole. This rapid expansion seems to have alarmed the powers-that-be, and various surreptitious, administrative attempts at capping shooting emerged in the form of police policies. We've mentioned attempts to eliminate collecting as a good reason; investments and heirlooms were similarly sneered at. Trophy-of-war certificates became limited to the person whose trophy it was, so families with such souvenirs were expected to part with them when the hero died.

The Metropolitan Police were refused permission (by the Home Office) to add .223-calibre Ruger Mini-14 rifles to their arsenal. The Met's firearms department promptly decided that, if they couldn't have them, neither could anyone else in London, thus starting a long battle whenever somebody applied for a .223 rifle variation there. Difficulties like this were unevenly distributed across the country. Each police force developed its own interpretation of the Home Office guidance and cobbled up its own public policies as it went along. None of it had the force of law, but might made right.

Here's just one example of inconsistency. Home Office guidance said that a target shooter would require authority to possess 1500 rounds of ammunition, and would want to acquire 1200 at a time. The Metropolitan Police interpreted this as 'rounds per calibre': so a certificate holder with fifteen different firearms might well be authorized to hold 22,500 rounds of ammunition. West Midlands police interpreted this as 'rounds per person'; so someone in their area with the same fifteen firearms might be authorized for only 100 rounds for each. Naturally, this varied *within* police forces as well; more experienced and active shooters were generally given greater allowances. The whole thing had, and still has, a dreamlike aspect in any case, as target shooters, particularly those who used .22 weapons, could buy and keep ammunition at their clubs, if they had adequate storage. These purchases don't appear on their certificates.

Another committee: a little transparency, a lump of fatuity

In 1985, the Home Office convened yet another in-house committee to review the situation. The upshot was that their guidance to the police would be revised and published, so that those it affected could, finally, read it in non-pirated form. They also came up with a really convoluted and supremely bureaucratic wheeze—land inspections. The supposed 'problem' was that deer stalking (in particular) takes place in counties with wide open spaces and deer, whereas most deer stalkers live in counties where there are houses to buy or rent. Because certificates are issued by the police where the person lives, forces such as the Met in London were authorizing their residents to buy rifles that they'd then use in other counties, such as Norfolk or Devon, or in other countries, such as Scotland and Sweden.

The land inspection charade was dreamed up so that the Met could notify the chief constable of the area where the stalker intended to stalk, and ask if the land was safe to shoot over. (Never mind that Prince Albert and his ghillies and everyone since had thought so.) In effect, it was a way of giving the local police the vital intelligence that yet another rifleman was coming to their area to spend money in hotels and restaurants.

One land, one law: and fifty-odd police forces being territorial and awkward.

CHAPTER FIVE

BUREAUCRACY ON THE RAMPAGE

THE HOME OFFICE circulated its revised guidance to interested parties—police forces and shooting organizations—in 1986, and it was still under discussion when the Hungerford murders took place in August 1987. The Conservatives had been in government since 1979 and had been re-elected in June of that year. They had no plans in mind for new firearms controls, and such discussions as had involved politicians over the preceding few years had focussed on the problems caused by the way the police were administering firearm certification. When it transpired that the Hungerford killer Michael Ryan had his guns on a certificate, Home Secretary Douglas Hurd quite quickly said that the public had no confidence in the system. He had personal experience of it, having for some reason failed to renew his own shotgun certificate in 1975. That had set him back fully £5 on conviction.

Before long, Hurd's officials had him strapped back in harness; then they launched a series of proposals for new prohibitions. On 24 September 1987, speaking at St. Edward's School, Oxford, Hurd said that public opinion in the wake of Hungerford had made him "more ambitious"; and that he was confident that proposals shelved as long ago as 1973 could now be reintroduced. And what came out, as a Firearms (Amendment) Bill, was essentially the Green Paper of 1973.

Since 1968, the law has recognized three classes of small arms: section 1 is firearms, as defined in the 1968 Act, section 2 is shotguns, as defined, and section 5 is prohibited weapons, as defined. The 1988 Act reclassified various firearms. For instance, a Remington 1100 shotgun might be a section 2 shotgun, or a section 1 firearm, or a section 5 prohibited weapon, depending on its magazine capacity, barrel length, and overall length. At least it was easy to sort out with a ruler. Less easy to deal with was the ambiguous phrase 'rifle includes carbine' in the 1988 Act. That led to a spate of court cases, as publicly-funded sophists tried to extend the scope of the prohibited-weapons class by prosecuting certificate holders and dealers. In truth, this was largely a job creation-and-maintenance scheme emanating from the Forensic Science Service. It was duly noted that their evidence about some firearms changed over time, as they struggled to find a form of words that would pressure the Crown Prosecution Service into launching indictments at hitherto 'authorized persons'.

Much of that bureaucratically-inspired crime wave was still in the melting pot when Thomas Hamilton slaughtered 16 schoolchildren in Dunblane in 1996. However, the Forensic Science Service didn't drop its hair-splitting agenda with the passage of the 1997 firearms amendment Acts. The basic method was the same—firearms moved within the classifications that had been around for decades. The Conservatives had put fullbore pistols into section 5; the incoming government extended this to .22 pistols.

That's the law: now let's have some nice juicy policy

New guidance followed in 2002, rounding up most of the policy changes of the previous decade or so and creating some new ones, such as the way they silently dropped any mention of vermin control as a 'good reason' to own a section 1 repeating shotgun. This wasn't a change in the law, of course, just a change made by government hirelings in the course of trying out new ways of not doing their jobs. If you already have a section 1 shotgun, the police will renew your certificate for that purpose, but they'll blank any newcomer, telling him it's not a good reason. No change in the law was necessary, just a change of policy in an unpublished document—which one witness to the Home Affairs Select Committee said should be given statutory force so that the courts would stop ignoring it. The courts would pay more attention to Home Office guidance, we think, if it reflected the law more accurately and was less bent to bureaucratic whim.

It's worth repeating that it's not only legislation that changes the way in which the shooting sports are affected by government; it's also surreptitious policy shifts like this. Take for instance changes to the way in which the Home Office expected approved shooting clubs to operate; this has had a significant impact on these clubs.

The first major shift followed the 1988 Act. Up to that point, approved clubs were free of much of the bureaucracy surrounding firearm certificates. The 1988 Act changed Home Office approval from a general approval, as set out in 11(3) of the 1968 Act (which was repealed), to one in 15(1) of the new Act. That specified which types of firearm the club could use; these were full-bore and smallbore rifle and pistol. So, at a stroke, clubs were no longer able to provide shot-gun facilities under their exemption, and the position of muzzle-loaded smoothbore muskets became yet more ambiguous.

Clubs could no longer 'drill' either. At first sight, this didn't seem to matter. But eagle-eyed members of clubs that enjoyed charitable status, because their constitutional objective was to assist in defending the realm in times of peril, saw it differently. To them, this looked like the work of a devious lawmaker intent on obliterating any remaining link, even a semantic one, between shooting clubs and the 19th-century volunteer rifle regiments—the militia. Their forebodings proved to be justified. But in any case a firearms 'drill' is any use of a weapon other than firing it, so emptying the ammunition out, easing springs and showing 'clear' is a drill. Then there are malfunction drills, cleaning drills and so forth. Clubs mostly got around this by dropping the word 'drill' from their constitutions and noticeboards and calling these procedures something else instead. Some of the older and bolshier members wondered out loud if the realm deserved defending, if it was so keen to separate its rulers from the ruled.

More squeezing—but still the pips don't squeak

The 1990s saw a further tightening of bureaucratic control of shooting clubs, in the wake of several incidents that caused the media to cluck and squawk. These made it harder for a newcomer to find a club and join it, and there were longer probation periods, limited access to training, and more police intervention. Club secretaries had to give police details of applicants wishing to join, whom the police could blackball without giving a reason. Clubs also had to log the attendances of each member and the particulars of which firearms he or she used, and had to report dormant memberships when they became apparent. Changes in the way the Charities Act was applied meant that—as the eagle-eyed had feared in 1988—clubs were no longer eligible for charitable status; losing it reduced their income.

The 1997 Acts further limited the approval of clubs to what few weapons were left to them; club approval after 1988 had ceased to cover smoothbored muskets, such as reproduction Brown Bess flint-locks, since they count, legally speaking, as shotguns. The option of providing facilities for, and thus managing, large areas of shooting for which the guns are still legally available has been taken away from clubs who want 'approval' from the Home Office.

Our best guess as to the reason for erecting all these obstacles is that it makes clubs less viable financially and training with firearms harder to get. We can't think of another reason why Home Office-approved clubs, the membership of which are all authorized persons, should be prevented from allowing their facilities to be used by people—again all authorized persons—who want space in which they can practise or compete with muzzle-loaded smoothbore guns, shotguns and section 1 repeating shotguns.

The mass of the great unregistered

Shooting sports in the UK reached a zenith in the mid-Eighties, reflecting the general well-being of the country. A recession followed on the heels of the 1988 Act. It may have been coincidence, but the gun trade was certainly the first into recession and the last out. The sport itself has never really recovered. Most types of firearm in use in 1985 are now prohibited to UK certificate holders, and clubs operate under very tight bureaucratic restraints. Despite all the regulation and regimentation, two spectacular firearms incidents made national news in the summer of 2010, when Derrick Bird in Cumbria and Raoul Moat in Northumbria went on their rampages.

Derrick Bird had had a shotgun certificate since 1974 and one for firearms since 2007, for pest control on private land. That he had guns at all was something that remained between him and the police. He was seemingly unknown to the sports shooting community in his area. He wasn't in the local rifle club, nor was he known to any of the local firearms dealers we spoke to.

The same could be said for Raoul Moat, except that he didn't have any certificates. Shortly after being released from prison he armed himself with a sawn-off shotgun, to wreak revenge on his former girlfriend, who'd told him she'd taken up with a policeman. None of the existing firearms controls prevented that happening, or could have. That there are unregistered guns out there for the Raoul Moats of this world to get hold of is without question. In 1988, using research published by Dr A B Bailey, Michael Yardley estimated that the unregistered pool of firearms stood at about 4 million guns.

That number was extrapolated from Metropolitan Police figures showing an average of 2000 guns handed in to them annually, mainly as deceased persons' effects. Their area records 100,000 deaths a year. In round figures, then, 2 percent of London deaths result in a gun going into the police. If you took the view that all deceased persons' guns are handed in, you're looking at a possible 2 percent of the population with a gun. A national population of 50 million (in the 1970s) equals a million unregistered guns. But, and it's a *big* but, we know that not all guns that change hands when their owners die go to a police station. They also turn up in the gun trade, in auction houses and in pubs. Some are undoubtedly kept by the next generation.

Compliance rates for acquiring a shotgun certificate in 1968 have similarly been estimated at between 10 and 25 percent.* With this in mind, Michael Yardley settled on a generous 25% compliance rate for handing in deceased people's unregistered guns. That equates to 8000 guns per 100,000 deaths, or 4 million guns in a population of 50 million—and nearer 5 million for today's population in the UK. Note that if the compliance rate is in fact as low as 10 percent, there would be more than 10 million guns in the unregistered pool.

Even 4 million is more guns than were on certificates at the time. That pool gets deeper with each turn of the screw of regulation and restriction, from the requirement to get a certificate for your Great War souvenir in 1920 to the requirement to get a certificate for your air cartridge revolver in 2004. Each time a new edict comes along, most owners—we reckon that even the 1997 handgun ban saw only 25 percent compliance—don't comply, or are obstructed by the issuing authority refusing them authority to keep what they already own.

We should comment about what's in that pool. At its simplest it consists of firearms that were legally owned prior to a change in the law creating a certificate requirement and firearms illegally imported since import licences became a requirement. You can expand that by thinking of firearms issued to the military, militia, police, and nightwatchmen, but not returned to store, hobby gunsmithing efforts, and so forth. The majority that we have seen filtering into the trade (the trade's guns are unregistered *per se*) have been pistols and shotguns. Fewer pistols have turned up in the trade since 1997—most gun dealers can't handle them because they are now prohited weapons— so unwanted pistols that don't get parked on the police are presumably still knocking about somewhere, off-ticket.

So that's where we are in 2011, and it's a far from ideal place: it's a mess. As we will show, it's a mess by design, not accident.

---

* At the time of the change all the people with shotguns would have found out about the new requirement at their local Post Office, which for months had notices up about getting the new shotgun certificate from the police. Despite all that publicity, take up was still poor, at best. There was a strong feeling in the countryside that tools of the trade should have nothing to do with the police. If a more appropriate agency, such as the local council or even the Post Office, had issued them, the take-up might have been better. Twenty years later one certificate, at most, per farming family was the norm —ammunition could be bought without a ticket— and then only if that family needed one, such as to take a gun for repairs.

Chapter Six

Mr Vaz and the Gun Control Network

O N 15 JULY 2010 in the House of Commons, MP Keith Vaz (Labour, Leicester East) signed and posted an Early Day Motion, which said:

> That this House notes with concern that children under the age of 18 years are able to hold licences for shotguns and other firearms; further notes that a child as young as 10 years old was awarded a licence for a shotgun by Bedfordshire Constabulary, which granted 49 similar licences in 2009; believes that children of such a young age are not responsible enough to be expected to adhere to gun control laws as stringently as is necessary; and urges the Government to review legislation relating to the award of shotguns and other firearms licences for those aged under 18 years.

On the same day, as chairman of the Commons' Home Affairs Select Committee, Mr Vaz announced a new inquiry into firearms control. It would "examine whether or not there is a need for changes to the way in which firearms and/or shotgun certificates are issued, monitored or reviewed as a means of preventing gun violence."

Both the EDM and the terms of the Select Committee's enquiry revealed a marked bias, which is quite normal among politicians who usually base their opinions on ignorance. But Mr Vaz's committee had considered the subject before, so we have to suppose that his position is based on his interpretation of evidence he'd heard there. If so, he reveals himself and at least some of his ignorance—for there is no such thing as a firearm or shotgun *licence*: the relevant Acts provide certificates.

Mr Vaz's rather crude, if crucial, terminological inexactitude indicates that he takes for granted the principle of banging the drum for more restrictions for their own sake. His early day motion may reveal more than that he lacked the tact to keep his hand well-hidden. For, by a mysterious coincidence, his Select Committee's previous report on firearms law, published in 2000, had noted a call for a minimum age of 18 for the 'ownership, possession and use of guns of all kinds'. Part of a long list of trenchant demands, this came from the Gun Control Network (GCN), who had given oral evidence to the Committee, as they were again invited to do in 2010.

Start shooting early, and keep shooting often

The neurosis about people under 18 shooting is a hardy but pointless perennial. Under-18s have firearm and shotgun certificates because the law requires them to. That they do have them demonstrates that they are indeed adhering to 'gun control laws as stringently as necessary'. In any case, young people with certificates still have to be supervised by adults, who can be expected to adhere as tightly as necessary (although Mr Vaz and the GCN appear to doubt that). That the responsible adult has put his child through the process of getting a certificate is hard evidence of strict adherence to the letter of the law.

The need for juveniles to have a shotgun certificate arises simply because the 1968 Act allows a person who does not hold a certificate to borrow one only from the 'occupier' of private property and to use it on that property in the occupier's presence. Let's flesh that out. You go to a farm with your 10-year-old, a gun, and your shotgun certificate. You have permission to use the land—but that doesn't make you the occupier: so your boy can't borrow your gun. He *can* borrow the farmer's, but then the farmer has to be present to make that legal. The simplest legal solution is to get the boy a certificate: then he can legally use your gun on the land under your supervision.

At the back of this neurosis is the theory—which plagues no other sport, no matter how dangerous—that preventing people under 18 from taking part in shooting makes them less likely to enter the sport once they are old enough. It's a way of trying to make the shooting sports whither on the vine. It's not the certificates, or 'licences', that the GCN or the handful of MPs to sign Mr Vaz's EDM object to, it's young people having access to firearms and getting careful training to use them safely and responsibly.

The alternative, that they sit at home massacring thousands in computer war games and doing whatever they do to their minds in the process, is presumably more acceptable to MPs, although various witnesses to the Home Affairs Select Committee were also asked about computer games. In practice, the children who don't get trained to use guns with due care and attention are the ones most likely to fall foul of the law, such as by causing criminal damage with an airgun, or harming each other. It's not the certificate holders among the under-18s who shoot their friends and enemies with air guns, it's people who have not had the chance to learn how to use them safely.

A minimum age of 18 for a certificate works only if all certificates include a condition allowing the holder to supervise youngsters using his firearms. What doesn't work is 18 as an entry point to shooting. No other sport has such a limit, although we like the idea of not allowing anyone under that age to play football. Maybe they'd concentrate on learning to read at school instead. And besides, playing football, along with riding and swimming, and even fishing, results in more fatalities annually than 'legal' shooting.

Gun-control enthusiasts may respond by observing that there's a minimum age for driving. Which is true, but it's not the entry age for using the roads. Novice drivers have already been road users for years as pedestrians and cyclists. Those who survive the experience enter driver training with 'road sense' gained from a lot of experience. Shooting is the same: years of experience as a minor precede the step into certification. We are simply arguing, once again, for a level playing field. If you ban people from having anything at all to do with guns before they reach 18, you must logically ban them from other, more dangerous sports, and from using the roads. Oh—and from joining the Army, the Royal Navy, and the Royal Air Force as well. And, believe it or not, this is what the GCN advocates.

The Gun Control Network wants a lot more than that

When the Home Affairs Select Committee considered firearms law in 1999/2000, they were doing so toward the tail end of the really paranoid phase after the Dunblane murders of 1996. The GCN emerged in that period and for a time enjoyed Tony Blair's patronage. The source of its funding is obscure, but its public faces are Gill Marshall-Andrews (wife of Robert Marshall-Andrews QC, MP, Labour member for Medway 1997–2010) and Dr Mick North, whose knowedge of firearms appears to date from 1996, when his daughter was killed by Thomas Hamilton in Dunblane. As far as we can tell, the GCN has never had more than seven members. According to its Flickr page, the organization currently boasts all of four members, among whom Dr North does not feature. But one of them *is* Professor Peter Squires, of whom more later. We merely note here that Prof. Squires's intimate connection to the GCN somehow failed to be mentioned to or by anyone when he appeared as a witness before the Home Affairs Select Committee in 2010.

Addressing the Home Affairs Select Committee in 1999, and in addition to keeping those of tender years as far as possible from firearms, the GCN proposed

> the elimination of the separate licensing [*sic*] regime for shotguns, the prohibition of certain categories of firearm on public safety grounds, the prohibition of replica firearms, and the licensing [*sic*] of all air weapons and deactivated weapons. It further pressed for the release of safety audits and police inspections of gun clubs, and risk assessments of gun clubs and the domestic storage of firearms.

This is quite a shopping list for an unaccountable group that has conducted no independent research. The whole of their agenda faces in one direction—that of further restrictions on the law-abiding—i.e. that 10 percent minority of gun owners whose firearms are already registered—without the even slightest pretence that such measures will have any impact on the criminal use of firearms. We don't know whether the illiteracy in the above quote is the Gun Control Network's own or that of the Home Affairs Select Committee, but the references to 'licensing' suggest a rather slack approach to the topic. In passing, we wonder what 'certain categories of firearms' the GCN thought *could* be banned in 1999.

But let's take their proposed measures one by one.

Firearms certificates. We agree with disposing of a separate licensing (*sic*) régime for shotguns; one category of authorizing certificate—firearms—should encompass all lethal barrelled weapons from which any shot, bullet or missile can be discharged, be they shotguns, handguns, rifles or machine guns, or bazookas and grenade launchers, come to that. One category for all, to be available against separate certificates of competence in each area of interest.

Firearms are inanimate objects. Banning any one type on grounds of public safety is contradictory, as they are all equally harmless. What matters about a firearm is who's holding it and what they do with it. Looked at from the GCN's perspective, probiting the police from having firearms would save lives.

Replica firearms are not firearms, full point. Various people over the years have suggested a ban, but in reality there are only two options. One is to treat replicas as real—which they aren't—and then license them *as if* they were real, which they aren't. One might as well do the same with pedal cars. The other option is to come up with a form of words that makes producing or owning *a firearm that doesn't work* into a greater offence than producing or owning a firearm that does work. It's nonsense and always has been.

Sir Eldon Griffiths tried to find such a form of words in 1981, after blank shots were fired near HM the Queen at the Trooping of the Colour. He attempted to articulate what a replica firearm was—'anything that resembles a firearm'. If enacted, that would have prohibited photographs of guns. Sir Eldon quickly retreated from an indefensible position. Anyone taking up his fallen flag is merely exposing their own stupidity to the rest of us. Replicas can be made of wood, paper, plaster, plastic, metal; carved from stone, cast in resin. The most interesting aspect of this particular proposal is the mentality of people who worry about inert, inanimate objects. Not being doctors, we don't know what pills to recommend.

Deactivated firearms. Here we go again. Deactivated 'firearms' are not firearms, just as replicas aren't. They are inanimate, non-functioning objects from which no shot, bullet or missile can be discharged. If you create a licensing (*sic*) system for them, treating them as if their deactivation had not taken place, nobody would want them—they'd use their licence (*sic*) to get an actual firearm instead. The whole *point* of deactivating firearms is to make them safe for people to own, for their own reasons, as with replicas. The process turns them from inanimate objects into inert inanimate objects.

What about the risk that deactivated firearms will be *re*-activated? Sorry, but that's already a criminal offence. We should point out that anything made can be un-made and re-made. Consider motor vehicles: you can strip one down to the basic box and build it up again with new parts; you can cut the box in half, add a chunk and weld it up. But to attempt similar work on a deactivated firearm is evidence of criminal intent.

Air weapons. The position with airguns is more complex and starts with their definition. There are a number of firearms-lookalikes out there that project a missile; not being lethal, they can't be defined as firearms within the meaning of the Act. They include 'air soft', paintball guns, and things designed to use elastic bands as missiles. What we don't know is whether or not statistics on the misuse of such things is lumped in with airguns generally. 'Proper' airguns are lethal, barrelled weapons from which a shot can be fired with enough force to break skin. Pistols managing less than 6ft/lb of muzzle energy, and rifles making less than 12ft/lb are exempt from registration. If misused, these are still capable of causing criminal damage and harm to other people. We would quite cheerfully put them into a simple mix that called for a fit person certificate, security certificate and a certificate of competence. If there is a *straightforward* registration régime for airguns, it would highlight as suspicious those people who avoid it, at least when buying airguns for the first time.

Otherwise, there are two snags here. The first is that there are already millions of airguns in the country, and history tells us it's unlikely that the rate of compliance with a new registration system is going to be significant. Most people use airguns for plinking or to dispose of the odd magpie or rat, quietly, on their own property. Why should they bother to register? The second snag is that, under the current administration of the law, government is perfectly capable of creating a certificate requirement for airguns, but then the police will make it next to impossible to get one—rendering the whole exercise pointless except to those whose salaries depend on the extra work.

The release of safety audits and police inspections of gun clubs. Wearily, we point out that there is no such entity as a 'gun club'. The term, when used, usually refers to a shotgun club, which does not currently require Home Office approval and is outwith police checks under the 1988 Act. The Home Office currently approve fullbore and smallbore rifle clubs and loose ammunition pistol clubs. In principle, we think that any publicity given to such clubs by the Home Office would be a good thing, making it easier for people who want to join them to find one. There is a balance to be struck, however; the police collect sensitive information that is protected by the Data Protection Act, while the individual members are entitled to privacy under the Human Rights Act. So a lot of amending of primary legislation would be necessary to give clubs the public exposure they would all like.

Risk assessments of clubs and individual storage. Interesting. We suspect that they don't understand the difference between a 'hazard' and a 'risk'. Firearms are inanimate objects and present zero risk in storage. So there is nothing here to discuss.

The GCN have expanded on what they have in mind *à propos* individual storage. They'd actually like to see published a list of those who own firearms in each police area (pinned up in local libraries, we imagine). Their website suggests this wheeze was nspired by the law that makes information about your local convicted paedophiles available to certain parties. We suspect the GCN think shooters are a rung or two below paedophiles on the moral food chain.

But the GCN should be careful what they wish for.

One objection to this wheeze is that it would create easy targets for burglars and terrorists hoping to get tooled up on the cheap. Or would it? It's easy enough to turn this kind of bright idea on its head.

If everyone knows you own guns, why not advertise it? We would put a sign on our front door saying ARMED RESPONSE and one on the back door saying BURGLARS! IS THERE IS ANYTHING IN HERE WORTH YOUR LIFE? Advertising our interest in shooting like this would solve most of the current difficulties the public have getting into the sport in the first place. All they'd have to do is look up who shoots in their area and then make an approach to the nearest certificate holder, requesting an introduction to a shooting club. The involuntary masonic secrecy that makes shooting so hard to get into would be eliminated at a stroke. We might have to be a bit more careful when we answered the door, but our common-law right to defend life, liberty and property is intact. The burglars and terrorists we shoot are sent off the field with a red card, while those who want to get into shooting legally know whom to contact. What's not to like?

Want to catch more criminals? Pass a few more laws

Behind all proposals like the GCN's (and like firearms law in the UK as we know it) is the assumption that additional burdens on the law-abiding will make some difference to criminals and sociopaths.

They *would* make a difference, but not to criminals. They would make more work for public servants, securing their jobs in difficult times. This is apparent at the time of writing from the upsurge in activity in police firearms departments—inspired, no doubt, by near-universal criticism following the murders in Cumbria. The police are doing their utmost to make their jobs look essential, just when everyone else in government—and the taxpayers who fund it—is looking for savings.

New laws increase the crime rate. Any increase in regulation is mirrored by a consequent increase in convictions of people who fall short of the new standard. Or to put it another way, the unwary get caught by people desperate to catch other people out, in order to generate the kind of statistics that make them look necessary.

CHAPTER SEVEN
MISSING THE POINT IN 2000 AND 2010

T HE HOME AFFAIRS Select Committee's firearms inquiry in 2010 wanted—or so they said—to consider the possibility of 'improving' the firearm and shotgun certification system as "a means of preventing gun violence". To that almost certainly unattainable end, they proposed to focus on five points. These are bulleted below, with our gloss on each following after.

- *The extent to which legally-held guns are used in criminal activity and the relationship between gun control and gun crime, including the impact of the Firearms (Amendment) Acts 1997*

   They have to put it like this because it's only what they call 'legal'— that is, registered—firearms that the government can control. Everything else is beyond their control. Think about it. The statistics they published in their report were unhelpfully vague: what they thought they might prove is anyone's guess. The Committee nonetheless managed to convince themselves that the UK's 'gun controls' do make a difference to homicide and other violent crime featuring firearms. On the other hand, in the four years following the 1997 handgun ban in the UK, crimes involving handguns increased by 40 percent.

- *Whether or not the current laws governing firearms licensing are fit for purpose, including progress on implementing the Committee's recommendations set out in its Second Report of the 1999-2000 session*

   Our answer is No, they're not fit for purpose. What the Committee's question really means is: Is there anything that could have been done (about registered firearms, since they can't control the rest), if only for the sake of being seen to be 'doing something', no matter how inane?

   And the answer to that, too, is No.

- *Proposals to improve information-sharing between medics and the police in respect of gun licensing*

  This has nothing to do with spree killers, but can be read as meaning that there might be a way of keeping more people out of legal shooting if the authorities can put the right spin on certain medical conditions and thus stigmatize them further.

- *Information-sharing between police and prisons in assessing the risk of offenders who may have access to firearms*

  This was an implicit reference to Raoul Moat coming out of gaol and picking up a gun immediately. They could try making that more illegal than it is already. Soon after, Moat broke the law quite comprehensively by shooting one person dead and horribly wounding two others. All the controls in the world on legally-held firearms were unable to prevent that. Perhaps in silent and embarrassed recognition of this elementary truth, the Committee didn't address the point and its 2010 report makes no mention of it.

- *The danger presented by, and legislation regulating, airguns.*

  You could read this as 'the danger presented by regulating airguns'. That's not what they meant, but it is the unintended consequence of what they were thinking. Including airguns in section 1 was proposed in their earlier (2000) report, which they stopped short of repeating this time—possibly because air-cartridge revolvers have gone into section 5 since. And that was a right debacle—there were hardly any applications for certificates for them from existing owners, so another 100,000 'prohibited small firearms' are now swimming in the unregistered pool.

In all this, there were two or three elephants in the room to which both the Committee, and even the few firearm-friendly witnesses they called to give oral evidence, remained resolutely blind. There may have been a few chubby little calves in there too—a veritable herd. We'll throw some light those in the course of this chapter; but first we need to crank up our time machine.

Back to a future that didn't happen

As noted, one of the Select Committee's intentions was to consider progress on implementing the recommendations in their previous report on firearms law in 2000. So we thought we'd start by looking at that effort. The 1999–2000 session of Parliament started more than three years after the Dunblane massacre in March 1996 and two years after the consequent knee-jerk legislation (the two amendment acts of 1997) had obliged firearm certificate holders to hand in their pistols, generating claims in excess of £90 million in compensation.

This was bit soon after the new legislation, then, to see how it was bedding down, particularly with respect to the usual stated aims of reducing gun crime. Historically, every Firearms Act has increased crime, if only by changing the status of weapons that many people had acquired legally before the goalposts were moved (or nicked, by government hooligans). The brutal truth is that people will ignore a law they think is outrageously unjust or just plain stupid. Firearms owners are no different. The wonder is that so many obeyed.

The Committee's approach in 1999–2000 was pretty much to give the newly self-appointed anti-gun lobby a platform from which to tell the great and the good what miseries they could have heaped on law-abiding shooters, but had missed the opportunity to hit us with. Their report is publicly available, but here are a few highlights from the recommendations and conclusions. These started at (a), went through to (z), and then started again at (aa) and got to (rr) before they ran out of steam—no less than 44 gems of wisdom in all.

Shooting sports, bling, culture, and being 'too realistic'

At point (d) they "recognize that there is concern over developments in shooting which may foster a 'gun culture'." Whatever does that mean?

We think two separate points have been fused and confused in that short sentence. 'Developments in shooting' must refer to shooting sports enjoyed with registered firearms, while the phrase 'gun culture' was probably intended to conjure up the dubious praise that some rap musicians have heaped on carrying pistols ('prohibited small firearms') as *macho* bling.* If you try to read the sentiment as one, it's the equivalent of saying that membership of a school orchestra and possessing a musical instrument should—somehow—not be allowed to foster a musical culture. Hmmm. Of course, the shooting sports already form part of a perfectly legitimate *sub*culture of those interested in guns, one that runs from people who write and read books and articles about firearms in all their aspects without ever coming near a weapon of any kind, through active shooters, gun-smiths and manufacturers, and comes full circle to those who collect all manner of small arms but never shoot them.

---

* Para 50 of the report observes: "The Home Office indicated that 'gun culture' could be defined as the perception of firearms as 'a means of resolving differences through violence, fuelled in part by their depiction in cinema and literature', and understood that 'amongst criminals, the carrying of a gun and willingness to use it to resolve conflicts is a sign of status and a means of gaining respect'." Which is exactly what the shooting sports do *not* encourage. The conflation of the two in the report is gratuitous, nasty, and misleading.

The Committee was almost certainly ambushed here by the inimitable Gun Control Network, which (para 51 of the report) "raised... its particular concerns about the discipline of practical shooting, which they believed introduced *an unacceptable degree of realism* [our emphasis] into target shooting situations." These people really should get out into some realistic fresh air for once in their lives. And perhaps watch a 'practical' shoot. Not very realistic. Targets don't shoot back—not even blanks—or run about, bleed, or fall over screaming and writhing. Courses of fire may be quite complex, and may need to be memorized—which isn't how firefights evolve in real life. In the UK's heyday of practical pistol shooting it was a standing joke among more worldly-wise shooters that the kit (custom-made 'race guns' bulging with sundry sophisticated optics) was about as *im*practical as it could get for use in the street or on a battlefield. Today, 'practical' rifle and shotgun competitions use less fancy weaponry but, like the practical pistol shoots of yore, are fine tests of agility, speed, accuracy and tactical thinking. That is about as 'realistic' as they get, although they are of some use when out in the field after game. They certainly don't have much to do with 'resolving differences through violence'.

Fear of the future and a fondness for fossils

At point (p) we find the Committee getting twitchy about 'new types of firearm... which appear to circumvent the provisions of the existing law...'. They go on to specify 'long barrelled revolvers', thus ignoring the eternal verity that if you set a legal minimum barrel length, a barrel longer than the legal minimum is *de facto* legal. Shotgun barrels are not 24 inches long (and longer) because that's the way the trade and the public want them; they are that long because Parliament said they had to be. It's not as if firearms are like cars, in which a 70mph speed limit sign can be ignored at will by the driver. They go on to suggest that the Home Secretary should take steps to prohibit new developments in firearms technology (there hasn't been one for over a century), but in their excitement they forget to mention the compensation that would have to go with such a provision.

They really get into their stride at point (q), suggesting that a list of 'approved' shooting disciplines should be drawn up, and that taking part in *those disciplines alone* should be recognized as a 'good reason' for possessing firearms. We think we smell here the same rodent that had its ratty underwear in uproar over the allegedly excessive realism of practical shooting.

There have been previous attempts to restrict shooting sports by (re)defining what constitutes target shooting. At one point the ever-reliable Metropolitan Police decided that a certificate holder who did not enter competitions didn't have a good reason for possessing his firearms. The court put them right on that, but that hasn't prevented a continual chipping away at what 'good reason' means. Such a list would fossilize shooting.

One has only to think back a century to appreciate that most shooting disciplines have moved on in that time. Distances have got shorter, for example: in 1910, 200 yards was normal at Bisley for both revolver and .22 rifle shooting. 'Mad minute' musketry was all the rage: the shooter used a bolt-action magazine-fed rifle, and took as many shots as he could get off in 60 seconds at a target at 200 yards' range.* Figure targets were then quite usual, but in the 1980s largely faded away for fear of the politically correct, as in the Olympic pistol duelling competition. Bullseye targets were taken over from archery, which could be seen as ironic. Some 'bullseyes' are square with round rings, and some are oblong with elongated rings.

Clay pigeon shooting hadn't been invented in 1910, and over-under shotguns were new-fangled, rare and exotic. Shotgunners used to shoot at projected glass balls containing soot, feathers—whatever would highlight the airburst when the target was hit. Clay pigeons, a much more recent (and environmentally friendlier) replacement, used to be all the same; then along came bolting rabbits, mini clays, *battues*. Practical shotgun, also comparatively recent at three decades old, is a simple progression discipline in which the targets are static instead of flying about. The shooter follows a set path looking for the targets. That's the same in principle as walked-up pheasant or rough shooting after rabbits. Perhaps they should have called it 'clay walked-up pheasant' instead. Some of the targets used are clay pigeons, others are reusable metal plates or skittles.

Strangulation by any other name

Anyone trying to draw up a list for 'approval' is going to forget something. Chalk discs are used by .22 rifle clubs as reactive targets. We also use Polo mints—you should be able to get the bullet through the hole in the mint without damaging the sweet. We also use cherry tomatoes as targets sometimes for miniature-rifle 'Day of the Jackal' shoots (melons are simply too big at 25 metres). All these and other schemes and wheezes are used in introducing new shooters

---

* The record for the Mad Minute was set in 1914 by Quartermaster Sergeant Instructor Snoxall, who put 38 rounds into a 12-inch bull at 300 yards. The British Army's qualifying score for infantrymen was then 15 hits in 60 seconds on a silhouette target at 200 yards; scores of 30 and over were not uncommon.

to the sport while providing a bit more entertainment than do little black bullseyes, and to relieve the tedium for more experienced shots. There are any number of disciplines that *could* be developed for .22 rifle shooters. Standard rifle, based on UIT standard pistol, anyone? That already exists, thanks to some enterprising shooters in Scotland. How about a miniature Mad Minute?

Ossifying things as they stand now would also, no doubt, make it 'illegal' in some pedantic Plod's eyes to shoot at Polo mints (gosh, a real danger to public safety there), as well as unlawful for clubs and coaches to think creatively about training techniques and new courses of fire. Perhaps the genius who thought this one up was hoping that it would help the shooting sports wither away from sheer boredom.

Concocting a list of target shooting disciplines for approval would be like going through the *Kama Sutra* and deciding which positions should be 'approved' for sexual congress and which ones shouldn't. And we all know that the *Kama Sutra* doesn't comprise a complete list. We also know (from our Oxford dictionary) the legend that the 'missionary position' is so-called "because early missionaries advocated the position as 'proper' to primitive peoples, *to whom the practice was unknown.*" Emphasis ours. Sigh. We also observe that the invention of an anti-gravity machine would call for a whole new *Kama Sutra*, and might well inspire a few new target-shooting disciplines too. No doubt the Home Office would be urged by fans of heavy government to say a few words...

What was interesting, though, about the concept of strangling the development of target shooting is that it was about the only time that the Committee strayed into thinking about the people who use firearms. Most of the time they seemed stuck on worrying about the inanimate objects, as though owners are irrelevant to the problem— whatever you perceive the 'problem' to be. All we can deduce from this recommendation is that the Committee chose not to learn from multiple past mistakes. At least the Home Office had the good sense to ignore them on this and most other points they raised in 2000.

A sentimental journey into Toyland

At paragraph (s), our eyes misted over. They wanted the Home Office to come up with unambiguous criteria for judging the lethality of a firearm.

They don't say so, but what they're on about is the break point between toys and guns. Some very low-powered 'guns' capable of launching a projectile do so with insufficient force to harm anything—such as a spud gun. There are also air-soft and paint ball guns, which can hurt but have such low measured power outputs that they don't count as 'lethal'.

At the back of all this was a political conflict between two forensic science laboratories. In Northern Ireland, they'd calculated for a higher break point than in England. In effect, the English labs were trying to widen the scope of 'lethal' by scooping down into the toy market to keep conviction rates up. Whereas the Northern Irish lab wanted a higher point so that they could define crowd control devices such as rubber-bullet launchers as 'non-lethal' and so make rejecting injury-compensation claims easier. There is case law on all this, of course, but it doesn't rate a mention by the Committee.

In paragraph (u) they were worried about developing air-weapon technology. This one has quite a long tale behind it. It started when the Forensic Science Service administratively banned CO_2-powered pneumatic guns on the grounds that CO_2 wasn't 'air': it was a gas just like the ones generated by the propellant in a cartridge. That the guns using it were within the muzzle-energy limits for low-powered airguns, of course, escaped their tunnel vision. You could still possess CO_2-powered guns on a section 1 ticket, and some people did, for shooting UIT competitions (which allowed them), because they are recoilless. Then in 1997, the Home Office downgraded CO_2 pneumatic guns from section 1, treating them as airguns to avoid the ignominy of sucking them into section 5 along with machine guns and fullbore pistols.

The basic difference between an 'ordinary' airgun and a CO_2 variant is that the latter use what's essentially a soda-siphon bulb as their power source, while traditional spring and compressed-air airguns are essentially bicycle pump technology that have to be re-cocked for each shot. CO_2 guns can be built as repeaters, so we can imagine— not without some glee—the panic that gripped the Gun Control Network when they realized that these (very) low-powered CO_2 repeaters had been unleashed from section 1 controls. They may have been unaware that there had long been repeaters in the general airgun market, powered by air-cartridge systems, and more recent air-reservoir systems—wherein the airgun is pre-charged for multiple shots from a diver's bottle. The market moves on despite the Luddites.

First, identify your problem

At point (x) the Committee call for 'local strategies' to reduce the misuse of air weapons. They don't give us much of an insight into what they think the problem is, and without proper identification of the problem any 'solution' may miss the mark. In 1988, we went on a coach trip to Belgium for an automatic-rifle shoot. The driver mentioned that there was a police campaign to have coaches banned from the outside lane on motorways. Sure enough, it was only a matter of time before we saw a policeman on television saying that the time had come to ban coaches from the third lane. He was being interviewed in the (irrelevant, or what?) context of a coach that had capsized on a roundabout! So, if the problem of 'misuse of airguns' amounts to kids plinking with airguns in public parks, one solution is to provide facilities where airgunners can be trained to use airguns safely. If that's not the problem, the Committee's time would have been better spent identifying what it is, so that an appropriate solution can be developed.

Their twenty-sixth point was that airguns should be 'licensed'. (This seemed odd the first time we read it, since no other firearms are licensed in the UK. But then it dawned on us that the Committee has consistently referred to licences, licensing, *et al.* when they mean the system of firearm certification.) What we see in this recommendation is an unconsidered solution to a still-unidentified problem, arrived at in haste and bypassing any process of thought. This tendency is however entirely consistent with the UK government's approach to firearms legislation since 1920, so perhaps we shouldn't be so pained.

The system's broke, but let's not fix it

Paragraph (z) was not their finale. At paragraph (gg), they recommend that the police retain control of firearms licensing (*sic*) administration. That's interesting, since at (jj) and (kk) they are pushing for a national database of certificate holders and registered firearms. Both would easily be achieved if a *national* office issued certificates, but that's way too efficient and cheap for this lot. What they wanted and, as far as we know, what they got, was a duplication. Local records are held in 50-plus ivory towers on incompatible systems, and then that information is forwarded to a national database that costs millions. It will be completely redundant once the proper national system suggested in this book replaces the current mess. The Home Office itself proposed such a sysytem, to be called the National Firearms Control Board—*as long ago as 1992.*

That they felt the need to say that the Victorian system currently in use should be retained, reveals that they're aware everyone wants to improve and streamline it. But they don't want to see any change that might actually make the system better. That would mean a fight with that vast and vocal vested interest, the police 'service'.

Point (hh) was a recommendation that the Home Office guidance be updated (it was in hand at the time) *regularly* (which hasn't happened) and that 'chief constables make it a priority to ensure that the guidance is consistently followed'. The trouble with the guidance is that it's not law. It's often silent about simple matters of procedure, in effect leaving pitfalls into which anyone trying to do things properly may fall, and in many places it's in conflict with both legislation and case law. Anybody slavishly following the guidance is going to be led into error, so chief constables generally prefer to do their own thing, right or wrong. We will return to this point in later chapters.

The final one we thought we'd mention is the consolidation bill urged at paragraph (rr). The Firearms Act, 1968, is a consolidation Act. You don't put anything new into a consolidation bill: it's purely a drawing-together of existing measures into one Act giving each a new paragraph number. So why didn't the government do it? Chances are, the Home Office still have some unfinished business with us all and they want to wait for a 'suitable legislative opportunity' to get some additional measures through before consolidating everything.

The Government responded to the committee's 2000 report quite quickly, damning it with faint praise. And there things were left until 2010, when the Committee revisited the subject, only to find that the only implementations of 'their' recommendations had already been in hand when they met in 1999—the secret national intelligence database and a revision of the guidance. The latter came out in 2002 and has not been updated since, despite the passage of sundry relevant Acts in the interim.

Scene: Westminster, ten years later...

Looking at the Select Committee's conclusions in 2010, it's striking that they'd leapt to most of their judgements *before* taking any evidence. Take paragraph 2, where they make it clear that licensed (*sic*) firearms are not the problem in crime, and observe that "Mass shootings with licensed [*sic*] weapons, such as the terrible crimes perpetrated by Derrick Bird, also thankfully remain rare." Then they say that the fact that our spree killers used licensed (*sic*) weapons "should not be overlooked in any further consideration of firearms legislation."

This is rampant gibberish. At best it's handwaving, designed to give the impression not just that something *can* be done about spree killers, but *will* be done, through legislation. They miss the obvious— that the three killers had certificates issued by their respective police forces who complied with the defective guidance that they were obliged to follow. If we are to operate in a 'blame culture', responsibility has to rest somewhere.

It gets better. In paragraph 5, they say that ignorance of the law should be an excuse for both police and public getting things wrong, because the law's so complex. This is not an argument that has ever impressed a court, ignorance of the law being no defence. More helpfully, they think the law should be simplified and made clearer. Mercifully a solution is at hand—in this book.

Missing in inaction: a curious sense of justice

Then it gets worse again. In paragraph 9, they pick up on police evidence about prohibition of individuals, suggesting that wholly suspended sentences should be reasons to divest individuals of their licenses (sic—but we've made the point, and won't repeat it). It seems that nobody read the Firearms Act as part of thinking about how to change it. Currently, a sentence of three months or more prohibits a person from possessing any firearm for five years from release. A sentence of three years or more prohibits that person from possessing firearms at *any* time thereafter, although an application can be made to the Crown Court for the prohibition to be lifted.

Short sentences and suspended sentences don't count. That's all in section 21 of the 1968 Act. Of note is that it all revolves around the sentence, not the crime, and courts don't show mercy by suspending a sentence without good reason. There's no specific guidance from the courts about prohibition, but there is a considerable body of case law about which crimes merit adverse attention to firearm and shotgun certificates and which don't. We visit them elsewhere in this book but, in brief, a breach of the Queen's peace can cost you your shotgun certificate. 'Danger to public safety' means violent crime, preferably involving a gun; it's not firearms administrative offences, it's not non-violent dishonesty, it's not motoring offences other than two drink-drive convictions within a 10-year period. Own up on your application to killing or maiming through dangerous driving, though, and (who'd argue?) you won't get a ticket in the first place.

None of this case law rated any mention whatever in committee, and in paragraph 10 they praise the police for failing to be guided by the courts when considering applications. Here are their words:

> We understand that police licensing officers are now encouraged to take into account intelligence about criminal behaviour that does not result in convictions, as well as convictions resulting in non-custodial sentences, when considering whether or not to grant a licence: it must be made explicit in police guidance that officers are expected to take such behaviour extremely seriously, in particular cases of bindovers, arrests and police call-outs for domestic violence, and an accumulation of convictions for

offences whose penalty falls short of that requiring prohibition.

This is the way things really are. The police administratively prohibit people who want to be legal by ignoring the law as stated by the courts—and natural justice into the bargain—while the Select Committee scrutinizing these matters think that's a good idea, and don't chastise the police for bringing the law (and themselves) into disrepute. Can it get any more corrupt than that?

Probably. The Committee recognize that current police guidance is out of date, but seem not to know how inept it is. Then they go on to suggest that it should become a Code of Practice. To be that, however, it has to reflect the law accurately and, until it does, codifying it would make matters a lot worse. The model is the Highway Code. It won't lead you into error on the roads. You can trust it, but not the Home Office guidance on the Firearms Acts.

And it's not what you do, it's whom you know

One area of concern that appeared at several points in the Committee's deliberations was that the presence of licensed firearms in a home might escalate domestic incidents. The Gun Control Network mentioned a Canadian experience in which the murder of women with 'licensed weapons' had dropped by 40 percent after it became practice to consult spouses over the license application. What they don't say is what had happened to the overall murder rate of women in the same time frame. Without those numbers their point smacks more of opportunist statistical selectivity than a reliable demonstration of cause and effect.

What went unmentioned is the conflict with other legislation that will arise if the police approach third parties to make enquiries about an applicant for a certificate. We have already had problems caused by the police taking account of other members of the household, despite the 1988 Act's security requirement and the (albeit potentially questionable) judgement in *Regina v. Chelmsford Crown Court, ex parte Farrer* in 2000, which we mentioned in the Introduction. The case of *Dabek v. Chief Constable of Devon and Cornwall* ((1991 155 JP 55 1990) comes to mind.

Mrs Dabek had two guns on an old white shotgun certificate (which had no security requirement) issued in 1980, and no record of complaints against her. In 1988 her husband applied for his own shotgun certificate, which the police refused on the grounds that he had had two convictions for possessing drugs in the 1970s. On realizing his wife had a shotgun certificate they revoked it on the grounds that they had no means of insisting that her guns should be inaccessible to him. Mrs Dabek appealed, and gave assurances that her weapons would be kept in a locked metal box and the ammunition in a locked drawer. Despite this and the antiquity of her husband's convictions, the court found that because both she and her husband (according to the police) still associated with drug users there was some potential, future danger to the public. Possessing drugs—scheduled ones—may be reprehensible, but it is not a violent crime; and as far as we know the law is not, in principle, designed to deal with crimes that have not yet occurred.

This kind of difficulty was seemingly resolved by the 1988 Act, or more specifically the 1989 Firearms Rules, which provided a condition on shotgun certificates that the holder should secure them against access by unauthorized persons at all times when not in use. It is not clear whether replacement of the old white certificate with a photo one that included the security condition would have satisfied Devon and Cornwall at the time of the Dabek case or not, but what is clear is that the police have referred to this case on subsequent occasions—typically when a teenage son in the family comes to police attention—and used it to argue that firearms should not be kept—regardless of the level of its security, apparently—in a house where any member of the household is known to the forces of law and order.

The Select Committee, egged on by the Gun Control Network, appear to want to amplify the doubtful premises displayed in the Dabek case. If this catches on, the police will want to know who else lives at an applicant's address—but if they object to the character of any member of the household *they can't tell the applicant what the problem is because of the Data Protection Act.*

Then he appeals. In court the police are not entitled to withhold anything that they considered in the course of making their decision, says the judgement in *Kavanagh v. Chief Constable of Devon and Cornwall* [1974] QB 624. So they have to disclose it all, despite ACC Adrian Whiting's indication to the committee that in the course of processing a certificate application he becomes privy to, and may act on, information that he would not want to share with the applicant.

The police would face the same problem if someone appealed the refusal or revocation of a certificate when the police have acted on the grounds quoted above in the discussion (pages 75–6) of paragraph 10 of the 2010 report, such as "an accumulation of convictions for offences whose penalty falls short of that requiring prohibition". As things stand, certificates are being refused for reasons of dubious legality, sometimes beyond the control of the applicant: which would seem to set up a further conflict between the Firearms Act, as implemented by the police, and human rights legislation.

The latter has yet to be addressed by those currently dealing with firearm and shotgun certificates. The 2002 Home Office guidance to police makes one mention of the possibility that Human Rights legislation has to be considered, and then goes on to ignore it throughout the remainder of the document.

So there's plenty to sort out, and most of it went over the Committee's heads. Vague calls for 'tighter' restrictions, for example, went unchallenged. Historically, every restriction on firearms has been financial, limiting them to the rich, or the upper classes if you will. That concept was holed below the waterline by universal suffrage. Any restriction you now think of will likely conflict with other legislation. Imagine restricting firearms certificates to people over 30, or to women only, or to British-born applicants. The potential for disaster is all too obvious.

We still think it strange that of all the millions of firearms in the UK, the Home Affairs Select Committee confine almost all their intended 'do somethings' to that tiny minority of the guns that are already regulated. Truth is, tighter restrictions are not the answer. The current system recognizes about 2 million firearms and shotguns, which is, at best, 10 percent of the national hardware stock. What is needed is a system that includes more of what's out there.

The medical profession isn't buying it

The Committee wanted to "improve information-sharing between medics and the police in respect of gun licensing". They had thought of getting closer to confidential medical information years ago. When they raised it in 2010, they ran into a wall of resistance from representatives of the British Medical Association. We are not prophets, they said. Mental conditions don't follow the predictable paths that physical conditions do. Well, we know some do: bereavement is a process that takes about a year to get through, unless you get into blaming others for your bereavement and spend your life trying to do something about the people you blame for your misery. Then you find yourself suffering from an unresolved bereavement complex, and the outcome is much harder to predict than it would be if you had regained a balanced outlook.

The bottom line is that the medical profession remains cautious about the Select Committee's agenda, and justifiably nervous that greater access to our medical records by the police might be abused.

It's also worth reminding everyone that none of the UK's recent spree killers had any history of mental illness and none was diagnosed by their GPs, so this proposal is not directed at any known problem. It's just another solution in search of a problem.

As we noted at the beginning of the chapter, the Committee didn't delve into the question of ex-prisoners getting guns at all; probably because there's no bureaucratic solution to be had. The obvious solution is to protect people at risk. The police have tried to make that into their selective monopoly. Monopoly, because they don't want anyone but themselves exercising the common-law right of self defence; and selective, because they can't provide as much protection as would be necessary. So unless you're Salmon Rushdie or royalty, they haven't got the resources to protect you, and they'd rather you died than had the means to hand to protect yourself.

A large grey creature with a tail at each end

What the committee avoided altogether here was one of the bigger elephants in the room: the fact that the whole of the jobs-for-the-boys system of regulating firearms in the UK applies only to firearms held for reasons *other than* the defence of life, liberty, chastity and property. These laws do not affect your common-law rights. Rather bizarrely, the people who understand this best in the UK are criminals. Most people with, for example, 'illegal', unregistered handguns in the UK are businessmen protecting their interests. They are, broadly speaking, unchartered chemists involved in manufacturing and the wholesale and retail distribution of certain popular, albeit definitely illegal, 'substances'.

At the retail end of the market, guns are largely worn as bling, making a statement of identity and attitude. Further up the market, guns have a real use in ensuring fair play. The illegal drugs industry obviously has no recourse to any of the UK's laws or law-enforcement agencies. They have to make each deal in their own way, and show potential business partners that they are serious about getting a fair exchange of goods for money—and that they would rather kill trying to complete the deal than die trying to do so.

We do hear of drug-related shootings in the press from time to time, but despite the illegal drugs market being reportedly huge, the UK's firearms homicide rate remains stubbornly low. Essentially, the murder rate with firearms has not changed significantly in 50 years, despite the increase in the population. One has to look at the figures in a way that the likes of the Gun Control Network and even the allegedly impartial Select Committee choose not to.

In 2008/9, there were 39 firearms homicides in the UK, of which four were committed with a registered weapon. Assuming (we're not told) that these involved four separate murderers using four different guns, that means 0.00019 percent of registered firearms were radically misused that year. For some reason this minuscule figure does not reassure those with an undue fear of inanimate objects—the technical term is *hoplophobia*, in the case of guns. For as the Gun Control Network assured the Committee—who were impressed enough to quote them in their report—"licensed weapons... *are* part of the problem." But they did not define "the problem", beyond implying their own degree of irrational phobia.

We can't be sure what percentage of *people* with registered firearms committed those four murders, because a fair proportion of them have both section 1 and section 2 tickets, and the figures don't tell us how many. Even if you assume that everyone with registered firearms has two tickets, our presumed four murderers represent 0.00086 percent of registered firearms owners—a number not usually regarded as especially terrifying. The murders themselves represent 0.16 percent of all homicides that year. Homicides with unregistered weapons amount to 5.4 percent of the total. We know with some certainty that there are *at least* twice as many unregistered weapons out there as there are registered ones. The figures *suggest* that those toting them are rather more likely (nearly 34 times as likely) to use them with evil intent, or in self-defence, than those who have registered their guns.

Looked at in perspective, you can reckon that you have about one chance in 92,000 of being murdered in the UK, and about one chance in 1.7 million of being shot with an 'illegal' firearm. If your profession lies outwith the law, it hardly needs saying, your actuarial position is likely to be rather more precarious. All the more reason, perhaps, to exercise your common-law right to keep and bear arms for your defence. According to rumour, even the police accept that, and don't prosecute villains who have the wherewithal to justify their carrying unregistered arms on those grounds.

Our point is… Oh, look, another elephant

Our Committee, however, managed to avoid the common law and its implications altogether, so we'll set them out here for them, in terms that should be clear even to the meanest intelligence.

The Firearms Acts in the UK do not affect the citizens' common law rights as enshrined in the Bill of Rights.

The Firearms Acts have not been amended to recognize citizens' rights under the European Convention on Human Rights (1966) and the Human Rights Act (1998). This is the next egregious pachyderm grazing in the Committee's chamber.

The handgun ban in 1997 was a mistake, and was followed by a wave of increasing firearms crime over the next seven years.

Spree killers always—in the UK at least—act only when they are certain there will be no armed interference.

Bad guys prefer one-sided gunfights. Just ask the police.

You can either have a permit scheme for people to own handguns legally, or put up with the fact that it's legal anyway under the Bill of Rights.

If you have a scheme whereby people—very thoroughly trained people—who own handguns can carry them discreetly, no robber, drug dealer or spree killer can act violently towards the public without fear of an instant reprisal. That's called 'behaviour modification'.

Essentially, the handgun ban in Britain is unsustainable. So something has to be done if the government wants to retain some control over the situation. From the sporting point of view, it needs doing fairly quickly to accommodate the 2012 London Olympics.

A prohibition on something, anything, means that there is no control over it. It's an *abdication* of responsibility. The corollary is that if there are no controls over something, no responsibility has been taken by the powers that be. The firearms debate crosses all three areas—the uncontrolled, the regulated and the prohibited—and the government is not distinguishing, either in their statistics or their tiny minds, one from another.

An interesting witness we'd like you to meet

The Select Committee's 2010 report cited Professor Peter Squires of Brighton University so often that one began to gain the impression that they were unusually fond of him. What he had to say in his evidence struck us too, as did what he did *not* say about himself. So we thought we'd give him a spot on stage here too.

Prof. Squires kicked off with the assertion that firearms offences were under-reported. There were, he said, some 55 offences that could be committed before a firearm was even pointed at anyone else. We know a bit about that. We know of certificate holders prosecuted for having a few rounds over their prescribed limit, for transporting guns to their range in precisely the way recommended by their local firearms officer, for 'allowing' unauthorized persons access to their ammunition (the scrotes broke into a locked, alarmed car), and many another heinous crime of like nature.

So we would be the first to acknowledge that with such restrictive firearms legislation currently in place, it's very hard for people to avoid falling foul of the *administrative* aspects of the law in some respect, whether it's a lapse of security, such as by taking a gun out to use, or some other wickedness. None of these offences in themselves constitute a danger to public safety, of course, unlike (in many circumstances, but not all) pointing a firearm at someone. Most of them are about equivalent to innocently parking on a double yellow line in the dark—an expensive mistake if you get nabbed, but not actually *dangerous*. Truck drivers, we recall, can commit 2000 offences before even getting behind an HGV's wheel. You might think the transport industry is over-regulated. Or maybe it's just that firearms legislation has a lot of catching up to do. Either way, one broken lightbulb doesn't make a vehicle's driver dangerous, or drunk, or dishonest.

Prof. Squires complains that "even simple illegal possession of a firearm... is not recorded as gun crime in the Home Office statistics." Perhaps that's because the guns in question haven't been misused: any more than a truck driver has misused his truck when a lightbulb blows. It's presumably this kind of 'crime' that justifies Prof. Squires in saying that "most gun crime in Britain is committed with weapons that are licensed or otherwise legal." There is another explanation, of course: registered firearms feature in a disproportionate number of offences (however minor) because they are actually being used regularly, and liable to scrutiny, whereas most of the unregistered pool is in storage. But you see the cast of mind, and where it's heading: any twisting and shuffling of the figures is acceptable if it helps to demonize registered guns and their owners.

Never trust a pedant with an agenda

This would have been a fraction less obnoxious if Prof. Squires had defined his terms properly, and even got some of his 'facts' in order. Paragraph 19 of the 2010 report informs us that the Professor

> told us that he had logged 44 domestic firearm incidents between 1 January 2010 and 30 September 2010 that were reported in national and local media, comprising nine murders, nine attempted murders and 23 other incidents involving threats, wounding, assault or Actual Bodily Harm, and animal cruelty. Sixteen of the incidents involved low-powered air weapons, *which are legal by definition*, and fifteen involved shotguns, one-third of which he estimated would be likely to be licensed.

It's hard to know where to start. It's *all* sloppy; and no real scholar would rely on media reports for evidence. The italics are ours—airguns are not legal *by definition*, although they are, if within legal power limits, exempt from certification. It's outrageously presumptuous to say that they are 'legal', given the connotations that that carries in this context. An airgun is legally owned only if whoever's carrying it is over 18, hasn't stolen it or borrowed it without permission, and it belongs to someone (who's also holding it when the music stops) who is not prohibited under section 21 of the 1968 Act. It's only legally carried in public if it's securely cased so that it cannot be fired.

The estimate that one third of the shotguns were 'licensed' is also questionable, on two grounds. *None* of them was licensed: as none can be in UK law. And how did Prof. Squires make this estimate? How could he possibly know? If the Professor is prepared to be pedantic about his 55 'gun crimes', he should learn to be pedantic with the rest of his terms, and use them precisely. Of course, all this managed to pass the Committee by. So did something else.

For all his assiduous mangling of facts, Prof. Squires managed to omit one very interesting one. It turns out that he's a member of the Gun Control Network. That illustrious organization already had two witnesses giving evidence to the Committee. Neither claimed him as one of their own. Was any of the Committee aware of the connection, and alert to the impression of bias it gives? If they were, did they care? Enquiring minds would like to know.

Some lessons in how to blur an issue

Flying under their own flag, the Gun Control Network had their own spin on deaths involving firearms. According to them, "between January 2009 and March 2010 fourteen people... died in 'apparent domestic shootings', at least five of which... involved a legally-owned shotgun." [Paragraph 18] Most homicide occurs within families. Anyone familiar with *King Lear* knows that family conflicts are emotionally among the most intense of all. Callous as it may sound, we have to wonder whether the victims of these domestic disputes would have died regardless of the available hardware. *The trigger does not pull the finger.* The notion of weapon substitution simply doesn't cross the radar here, as tunnel vision fixates on the object used, not the prime movers in the dispute. The GCN also lumped suicide (which is not a crime) into their rhetoric, and generalized that the majority of mass killings around the world involve legally-held weapons.

That's true, of course. Most such events involve legally held firearms—in the hands of government employees doing the bidding of their governments. Whether at Babi Yar in the Ukraine, Lidice in Czechoslovakia, Sharpeville in South Africa, My Lai in Vietnam, Waco in Texas... Governments also use other means, such as plastic bags in Cambodia and machetes in Rwanda. We could go on, but the key point is that the vast majority of mass murders are inflicted by agents of a régime on unarmed citizens. Which is why mass murders tend not to take place in well-armed societies, where the respect of public servants for the people they serve is more evident. And most mass murders by individuals, as we persist on insisting, take place in societies or in places where the perpetrators can count on little or no resistance.

Some last points missed in 2010

In paragraph 39, the Committee states that if Derrick Bird "had not possessed firearms, the killings would not have occurred." We've just covered one objection to that blanket assumption. We wonder, too, if this statement isn't a perversion of a remark by witness Dr Chrystie (whose daughter was injured in the rampage) that "if the late Mr Bird had not had access to firearms he would not have been able to use them." That is true. But it is *not* the same thing as saying that without firearms, Bird would not have killed.

If correct, that argument would sweep away more than a century of sociology. Emile Durkheim (looking specifically at suicide) demonstrated in the late 19th century that the effect of removing one means of killing is that people find another method. It is common knowledge that Bird's first few victims were targeted individuals who knew him. Once he had access to them, any lethal implement would have served his purpose. We do agree that the success of his random attacks on *later* victims did largely depend on his having firearms. Had Bird used some other weapon(s) for the targeted murders, he might have left the others alone. Equally, he might have run people over, given the opportunity, with his legal car.

In 2010 the Committee backtracked a bit from its earlier position on airguns. The ground is a bit marshy here, and they went too far last time in calling for them to be licensed. But, to be fair, airguns have been on the police agenda for over a century and the problem (such as it is) is still unresolved. To put that 'problem' in perspective, the following figures may help. Less than one in a thousand airguns was misused, and less than one in a million caused a 'fatal or serious' injury in 2008/9. Legally defining when a really low-powered airgun is a toy or is a weapon would make a difference to whether some people—prohibited persons and juveniles—have committed an offence or not, but, er, that's it.

It's not too hard to work out that a hand-held knitting needle is potentially more lethal than a low-powered airgun, so logic should lead us back to thinking about the person holding a weapon and what they might do, rather than focussing on the inanimate object. What the Committee were thinking about in response to the slaughter in Cumbria was made plain in the opening paragraph of their report, with its talk of "the dangers of firearms". And here we spy yet another of those elephants that crowded the Select Committee's room. Their focus on 'improving' controls, we thought, exposed their hand: they really wanted *more* controls, if they could find a way to conjure them up.

What they should have been thinking about was not firearms, but people with mass murder in mind. The Committee gratuitously hauled a number of Derrick Bird's victims to London to talk about a horrible experience that they might prefer to forget, but they invited *no one* with any expertise on spree killers to address them. That should have been their very first task, and they ducked it. They wouldn't have heard anything to reassure them, but they should have had the wit and good grace to seek out that kind of expert knowledge, of which there is no shortage. If they had listened to it, they could have shelved the rest of their agenda. That would have been refreshing to see, in politicians.

In the end, the Committee's position turned out to be something like: 'The effectiveness of current legislation is no reason *not* to interfere more.' The government's position might be: 'Various of our employees are looking to see if anything *could* be done to interfere.'

Which means that the government is complacent enough to leave the detail to the very people who caused most of the problems in the first place! And that means that virtually every recommendation in their report was a waste of paper and bandwidth.

PART THREE

Rethinking 'gun control'

The only power any government has is the power to crack down on criminals.
Well, when there aren't enough criminals, one makes them. One declares so many
things to be a crime that it becomes impossible for men to live without breaking laws.
Who wants a nation of law-abiding citizens? What's there in that for anyone?
But just pass the kind of laws that can neither be enforced nor objectively
interpreted—and you create a nation of law-breakers....
—Ayn Rand

It is wrong to represent bureaucracy as an evil contrived solely by socialists.
It is one of the evidences of original sin.
—Evelyn Waugh

I'm going to rub your faces in things you try to avoid.
I don't find it strange that all you want to believe is only that which comforts you.
How else do humans invent the traps which betray us into mediocrity?
How else do you define cowardice?
—Frank Herbert

CHAPTER EIGHT

THE LAW IS A MESS, AND IT KEEPS GETTING MESSIER

WHEN KEITH VAZ MP announced the publication of his Committee's report in December 2010, he said: "Current gun law is a mess—it needs to be simplified, clear, and consistent, to be properly understood by both those using firearms for legitimate purposes and those in charge of enforcing the law." That is surely true, but Mr Vaz scarcely scraped the surface of the problem. The truth is that the UK's current firearms laws are both inconsistent and profoundly illogical, are administered with an institutional prejudice, and (if that's not enough for you) have been unlawful, as well as unconstitutional, since 1998.

The third point is quickly addressed. We noted earlier that the Scotland Act, 1998, upholds the 1966 European Convention on Human Rights. The rest of the UK is covered by the Human Rights Act, 1998, which does the same thing. The UK government can't amend the European Convention on Human Rights, as they didn't pass it. The Convention makes a number of general points, but the key one for the 1968 Firearms Act is due process—the right to a fair trial. Nowhere else in UK law is the issuing authority of a certificate, or a licence for that matter, also the revoking authority. The significant fault line through the 1968 Act is that it makes the police the prosecutor, judge, jury and executioner in their own cause.

Our first point is clear to all except those who believe in magic, and think inanimate ojects have a life of their own—people like the Gun Control Network (GCN), who regard lethal weapons as if, like the animals on George Orwell's *Animal Farm*, some were more lethal than others. As Derrick Bird demonstrated all too clearly, a .22 rifle and a shotgun are just as deadly in certain circumstances as an AK47 assault rifle or a .357 revolver. But if, like the GCN, you would not-so-secretly like to see all firearms of all kinds taken out of private hands, you are at least adopting a consistent position with a kind of logic to it, albeit of an impractical and probably unconstitutional kind. Banning certain classes of firearm and not others makes no sense, and the UK is unusual if not unique among democratic societies in doing so. Loads of inanimate objects are potentially lethal: pencils, chainsaws, ladders, knives and forks, fan heaters, hatchets, cricket bats, bricks, cars, combine harvesters and swimming pools among them. Like rifles and pistols, they become lethal only through the agency—deliberate, stupid, careless, or accidental—of a human being. It is a curious fact, however fervently bureaucrats may wish it were otherwise, that human beings are not entirely predictable.

'Every possible difficulty should be put in their way'

That leaves the meat in the sandwich: what the current laws are supposed to do, and—the thing that impinges more on the people who want to abide by the law—the way they're administered by the police.

Currently, the system is being twisted in order to keep people out of it. Police forces spend a huge amount of money resisting a small number of applicants who, by definition, want to use guns legally. The objective is to keep the number of certificates down, imagining that this is, of itself, a good thing. As long ago as October 1982 an editorial in the *Police Review* articulated a view that has become still more ingrained over the years:

> ...we consider that the number of section 1 (i.e. ordinary rifles and pistols) firearms held in private hands should be kept to the absolute minimum. There is an easily identifiable police attitude towards the possession of guns by members of the public. Every possible difficulty should be put in their way.

We also have a copy of a letter, written in 2003 and signed by an assistant chief constable in Scotland, that concludes: "...it would seem that any action, which would prohibit access to firearms, whether restricted or not, is a positive step."

This kind of institutional prejudice can create real problems for someone who wants to be legal when a police officer or civilian colleague is making enquiries in connection with a certificate application. Combine this pressure, seeping down from 'authoritative' sources but with no basis in law, with what Home Office circulars say, the inaccuracy of Home Office guidance, and 34 separate pieces of legislation, and you get what we've got in the UK today.

The firearm certification system was introduced in 1920 to control or register newly acquired firearms that were not kept for defence of the realm or defence of life and property. That at once set up a false dichotomy and the potential for both confusion and meddling. It's arguable that a rifle used on private land is being used to defend property from the depredations of pests and vermin, which is a legal obligation, and so falls outside the 1920 Act. A rifle used to shoot invading deer only on farmland (as opposed to when stalking, which is a sport) may likewise fall outside the Act, but it may be equally serviceable in competition work on the range and, as such, would need to be registered. There is a huge variety of firearms manufactured that will suit an equally wide range of purposes.

Take shotguns, for example. Certainly handy for rough or driven shooting of small game, and mandatory for clay (skeet) shooting, they have also been seen service in various theatres of war. The first repeating shotgun, Christopher Spencer's 1884 pump-action design, found a niche in the security industry, from which it found its way into police and military service, as well as finding a home in rural pest control, some clay shooting, and practical shotgun competitions.

What really determines what a shotgun is good for is its ammunition. And shotgun ammunition fits shotguns: pumps, semi-automatics, over-unders, doubles and singles. It ranges from what's good for pigeons in barns, through loads for clays, to what's best for buck. Just a handful of specialist cartridges can be used only with certain types of action—most shotgun cartridges will work effectively in all types.

Which type someone chooses to own is, surely, a matter for that someone, not one for the fine distinctions beloved of bureaucrats, whose obfuscations and ambiguities provide fertile opportunities for the police to be awkward or, if they're feeling lucky, to prosecute.

The first problem is accountability—or lack of it

The law currently defines three classes of firearm—those falling to sections 1, 2 and 5 of the 1968 Act. Sections 1 and 2 are administered by 50-odd local police forces from their headquarters. Section 5 authorities are administered centrally from the Home Office. None of the people working in these systems is accountable within the meaning of the phrase intended by the current Prime Minister. Police employees are accountable only to their chief constables, and we don't elect them. Home Office officials are so sheltered from accountability that they were able arbitrarily to revoke the authority of the company that imports the TASER shotgun cartridges deployed (or not, as the case may be) in Raoul Moat's pursuit. They won't be accountable for the subsequent suicide of the supplier either, whose business they destroyed with a single-page letter.

At its simplest, our system of controls amounts to passing a character test and then having a good reason to own the guns you want. Everything over and above that is job creation by and for bureaucrats and police. The courts have said very clearly who should pass a character test, but the police (and the Home Office in its guidance to them) continue to ignore case law. Much of what these parasitic pen-pushers do is worthless. It doesn't prevent crime—although it might create some. Why do we say such irreverent things? Let's see how the system works under the present dispensation.

Imagine yourself escaping from the 'burbs to live in the country–side. You've found a nice rural property, with fields for the ponies, a small orchard, some barns. You will almost certainly have vermin in your idyll: pigeons and rats in the barns, crows and magpies, foxes and maybe deer in the fields and orchard. You decide a rifle or two and a shotgun will help you reduce their number. The logical place to get advice about dealing with these pests, the extent to which you should, and the kit to use against them, will be neighbours who have experienced and probably dealt with similar problems.

Learning to shoot the hard way

What is currently quite difficult to get, unless your neighbours are generous with their time, is practical help in learning to use a gun. In limited circumstances, you can borrow guns from neighbours and use them in the owner's presence, but only on his land. If you get him onto your land, he can do the shooting, but you can't. In such ways the law neatly makes it quite difficult for you to get the advice and experience you need to do things effectively yourself. Doing other-wise has you and your neighbour committing one, maybe two, of those 55 offences that can occur 'even before a gun is pointed at any-one' (or even at a crow), of which Professor Peter Squires is so fond. Apart from contributing nothing to public safety, what is so utterly fatuous about these legal booby-traps is that they are virtually unen-forceable, at least in the depths of the countryside. So people do what common sense tells them is safe, regardless. And while technically they make themselves criminals, the law slides further into disrepute.

There is a bit of a shortcut to be had in applying for certificates immediately. But if you decide you want a rifle or two but don't have much experience with them, what you supposedly need for the job is likely to be decided for you in police headquarters. Your neighbour may recommend something, but the police may well say it's too powerful for beginners—not that they're experts. Police 'knowledge' of firearms most often comes from not-always-reliable Home Office advice, not from being shooters themselves. And while your neighbours may have repeating shotguns for pigeons, the police will say pest control isn't a good reason to have one in your case.

So, access is difficult, and training is hard to find and restricted, because of what you can and can't do without a certificate of your own. Where training is provided, such as in clubs, another set of restrictions apply; the club secretary has to let the police know of your interest and wait to see if they will approve your probationary membership or not and then, once in, you can train only on firearms that the club is approved for. That's fine if target shooting and club membership is what you're after. But if you try using that as a prelude to independent pest control, it won't help you much beyond teaching you good range manners and the iron rules of safe gun handling.

How to simplify things: follow an existing model

Shooting is as wide in scope as driving. With a driving licence of the appropriate category, you can drive a moped, a motorcycle, a car, van, truck, large goods vehicle, articulated lorry, a bus, a bendybus, a steamroller, tractor, locomotive, or tank. What you do is get the basic (provisional) licence as your entry to driving, and then fill in the above categories by obtaining a certificate of competence from a testing station after appropriate training—usually from a proper school. It's a nice, simple model for dealing with people who want or need to take charge of potentially dangerous objects, and it's easy to understand and administer: something to follow, surely.

First things first. The provisional driving licence essentially does no more than register your intention to take training, and it's issued without quibble or qualm, unless a court has previously prohibited you from obtaining one. That's all anyone should need to start shooting—a certificate that declares he or she is a fit person to use firearms. And that's the point at which current police policy is at odds with both the law of the land and the decisions of the courts.

The fit-person or character test is already enshrined in legislation and case law. We look at this more closely in the next chapter. In summary, non-violent crimes don't count against you, and 'administrative' firearms convictions (such as for having a few rounds over the limit on your ticket) don't count. Some violence may be excused as long as guns are not involved. The police need to get themselves straight about all that, while for would-be shooters a straightforward criminal-record check would sort out the lambs from the foxes.

Many who are interested in taking up shooting won't know immediately which aspect of the sport they want to concentrate on; target shooters' clubs at least usually have a variety of kit for their members to sample. Others, like our-would be pest controller above, will already know which skills they need to develop, over and above making safe gun-handling second nature in all the conditions in which they shoot. In both cases, public safety and the Queen's peace will be better served in both the short and the long run by dumping the inane restrictions on who can shoot what, where, and in whose company, so that people can get the right training, in the field or on a range, with the maximum range of weapons and the minimum of pettyfogging hindrance.

Once you've got a certificate, you can still lose it

To get a firearm certificate you need to leap certain hurdles, and if you fall below those standards your ticket can be revoked. The law also provides further grounds for revocation—although at present this essentially gives more discretion to faceless and unaccountable officials, who may or may not decide to carry on liking you. You can lose a shotgun certificate (the *law* says) only if you demonstrate you're a danger to public safety or to the peace. Despite that, we know of no case in which someone has had a firearm certificate revoked but their shotgun certificate was not, despite the additional tests that a firearm certificate holder can be measured against. There are three grounds for revoking a firearm certificate—'unsound mind', 'intemperate habits', and 'otherwise unfitted to be entrusted with a firearm'.

The last of these—'otherwise unfitted to be entrusted'—rates a mention in the *Shepherd* case described in the next chapter. It's the first and so far the only case of record to distinguish between the tests for keeping a firearm and a shotgun certificate. In that case, the judge felt that concealing prohibited small firearms (handguns, to the rest of us) and lying to the police could be taken as evidence that Shepherd was 'otherwise unfitted to be entrusted' with section 1 firearms, but it didn't make him a public menace. So he kept his shotgun certificate.

On the other two, the courts have been silent. We think the key reason for that is because revocation letters usually parrot the whole law; so if you're both a firearm and shotgun certificate holder and some unaccountable bureaucrat decides that you should cease to be so, the letter you will get says that the law permits the chief officer to revoke your firearm certificate on the grounds of unsound mind, intemperate habits and otherwise unfitted to be entrusted and in the case of a shotgun certificate danger to public safety or the peace; and that the writer is satisfied that you should no longer hold certificates. What you don't know is whether the faceless one thinks you're as mad as a bag of badgers (or on what grounds), has spotted you in the pub, mildly tipsy at your own birthday party, or if your neighbour has seen you shooting at his deer across a four-lane highway.*

In practice, there is little point dwelling on the fine print of what these phrases in the Act might mean. If the police, whatever their real motives, want you out of the certificate system, they issue a generic letter. A court hearing an appeal under section 44 will largely be concerned with the overall justification for the police action, not the fine detail as to which category, if any, applies.

The real problem is that the wording in the Act, which on its face isn't unreasonable,, has become thoroughly discredited through extensive abuse over a very long period. It's also true that the police don't differentiate between the wordings for the two certificates—so we have the case of *Germain*, which revolved around a shotgun certificate, while the police action was based on an assumption of 'intemperate habits', which aren't grounds for revoking a shotgun ticket.

Madness is sometimes in the eye of the beholder

'Unsound mind' is a really tricky concept and needs thinking about carefully. The last Labour government went a long way in recent years to try to persuade the rest of us that mental illness is no more abnormal than a physical illness, and nothing to be frightened of. Clearly there are limits to that idea (as with homicidal schizophrenics who are inadvertently released into 'community care'), but the basic humane principle has considerable merit. That campaign was fronted by some well-known figures including David Blunkett, a one time Home Secretary, and Alastair Campbell, who was Prime Minister Tony Blair's official spokesman for many years.

Would you have taken Alastair Campbell's firearm certificate away on finding out about his mental difficulties, or was his condition of insufficient concern to merit such draconian action? He says in his

---

* The 1988 Act added a position, in section 12, by which, if "necessary for public safety", the police could also seize the holder's firearms and shotguns immediately as part of the revocation process. Since that option came into force, we have not heard of a single revocation anywhere in the land to which it has not been applied. It has also been applied to cases of refusals to renew, to which the Act does *not* extend the option, and it has been used to seize shotgun cartridges, to which the Act does not apply at all. When a source close to the most senior Home Office ministers remarked to us in 1988 that "the police are out of control", he knew whereof he spoke.

blog that he had a nervous breakdown in 1986 and bouts of depression have recurred since. If you thought his firearm certificate should go on 'unsound mind', given that his condition didn't stop him working closely with the Prime Minister, would you have left him his shotgun certificate, or would you have regarded his condition as evidence of danger to public safety or the peace?

How would you know anyway? In his report on whether Derrick Bird's certificates were properly issued, ACC Adrian Whiting suggests it would be a good thing if the police had greater access to medical records when issuing or renewing tickets. At the same time, he points out that Mr Bird had not mentioned any mental-health problems to his general practitioner (as Dunblane mass-murderer Thomas Hamilton also did not), so his file would have been empty.

There are two obvious objections to this notion of the police peering into medical records. One is that GPs are not psychiatrists; and the other is that policemen aren't psychiatrists. Police forces may consult medical personnel on their payroll, but are not obliged to by the 1988 legislation. This was a deliberate oversight; Douglas Hogg (then Minister of State, but now renowned for his clean moat; he retired from Parliament at the 2010 general election) said that the police must have unfettered discretion. Medical evidence is considered by the Driver & Vehicle Licensing Agency, in connection with driving licences. GPs have to tell the DVLA about certain conditions that may affect their patients' competence behind the wheel, and the evidence is then assessed at the DVLA by a doctor. In other words, by a qualified person who can understand the evidence, not a policeman. And certainly not a policeman with an officially-sanctioned agenda to keep as many qualified drivers off the road as possible.

Learn to live with it: no one can predict the future

The medical profession say they are not oracles, as BMA representatives pointed out to the Home Affairs Select Committee in 2010. Predicting the future is not possible in the light of vague, or even precise, evidence of a state of mind, whereas a physical condition will more probably follow a predictable course. It also needs repeating, apparently, that along with a raft of other recognized mental illnesses, a 'nervous breakdown' or a state of depression does not inevitably lead to a tendency to violent behaviour, toward oneself or others. And it shouldn't be forgotten that for some people, the pleasure and reassurance they get from shooting well (and the fresh air and exercise that may entail, if they go out after live quarry) may actually help them to make their way *out* of depression.

Our view is that if government seriously thinks mental health is an issue among shooters, the simplest way to deal with it would be to require a medical exam similar to that undertaken by heavy goods vehicle drivers, or the psychological test that the police use in selecting officers for firearms training. We're confident that it won't do any good but, if it makes politicians feel that they've 'done something', at least they'll move on to something else, and possibly—but don't hold your breath—they'll stumble across something useful they could be doing instead, such as abolishing the excise duty on diesel fuel. This book is packed with useful tips for politicians in that predicament.

The general view among certificate holders, we observe, is that the powers-that-be want to reduce their number and therefore, if the police had unfettered access to shooters' medical records, they would be hunting for yet more nit-picking excuses to issue revocations and refusals. As police officers are not, generally speaking, qualified psychiatrists, their lust to go snooping begins to look like just more evidence of their unsuitability to be the gate-keepers to firearms ownership. In answer to our questions above, by the way, we think that Alastair Campbell's condition was never serious enough to warrant intervention. Indeed any official acting intemperately could have made his delicate mental health worse, giving him something else to worry about that was beyond his control.

What shooters and would-be shooters are up against is that the basic character test that lets them go about their lawful business is administered by unaccountable people, in numerous offices up and down the land, who interpret it in their own way, which means inconsistently. That inconsistency is a major part of the mess that is firearms law and the way it's applied. By taking every opportunity to be pedantic or to meddle, the administrators have destroyed their own credibility; and they make matters worse every time they make a decision that fails to fit the framework provided by the law, the courts, or (most often) by logic.

CHAPTER NINE

WHO SHOULD HAVE GUNS —AND WHO SHOULDN'T?

T HIS IS A TRICKIER QUESTION than it seems at first sight, because of the common law. The 1688 Bill of Rights doesn't define what arms a person may keep and bear for his defence, so it must mean such arms as are available. As the right stands for all time, the precise choice of arms is left up to the individual citizen, or subject of the Crown. So the first question we should ask is whether we should have a system of registration and certification at all, given the common law right we have to defend ourselves, our property, our families, and others in peril of their lives.

Glorious as the thought is, we don't imagine that any bureaucrat is going to accept in principle, let alone practice, that his job is pointless and 'gun control' is a bad thing. Bureaucrats and police have spent decades developing this particular power base and making their jobs secure by dreaming up new restrictions, whether they work as advertised or not. And the current government seems content to let them carry on making the mess they've made even messier and more complicated. But we do think that, in a free country, such controls as affect us should be cost-effective, should have a measurable benefit, and should not conflict with other laws—the common law and the European Convention in particular.

The 1903 Pistols Act did not interrupt the right to keep and bear arms, as its requirements did not inhibit the buyer from acquiring whatever he wanted; at worst all he had to do was pay a tax, in the shape of a Gun Licence. In 1918 Sir Ernley Blackwell blithely imagined that his proposed firearm certification procedure would draw in everyone who kept firearms for lawful purposes; but he took no legal advice on the matter, and no one on his committee thought to ask if his proposals might be incompatible with the common law. But even with registration and certification, no one questioned the notion that a householder could continue to acquire arms for self-defence.

For decades, the police accepted self-defence as a 'good reason' for having firearms—until 1954, when the Home Office issued a policy statement (or edict, or decree) that chief constables should no longer issue certificates for that reason. Neither this policy nor the constitutional validity of certification has ever been properly tested before a court, so publicly at any rate their status remains unresolved. As we mentioned before, however, stories surface from time to time of police who, on apprehending armed citizens hefting (for example) substantial quantities of scheduled drugs without lawful authority or reasonable excuse, are very careful not to prosecute—for firearms offences—said citizens if they maintain that they are tooled up to the nines purely in the interests of self-defence. If accurate, such tales indicate that the powers-that-be want to avoid, if at all possible, the delicate position of the Firearms Acts coming under open, and perhaps unsympathetic, legal scrutiny.

For the rest of us, who can't afford to carry big bags full of dope around in order to justify the Desert Eagle under our armpit, the system is a fraction more fraught. When we apply for a firearms certificate, we have to satisfy our chief constable that we're 'fit' to own the firearms we want.

The way we live now

In theory, it should be fairly simple to set a national standard for this character test, and make it one that we can all understand. It should also have some basis in logic and be used to deal with real problems and not used to pursue some bureaucratic agenda aimed at disarming the populace.

Fortunately, the basic character test is already quite well defined by various court decisions and by the law. The Security Industry Authority use the same criteria in deciding who can or can't have one of their badges, and their system works quite well. In principle, everyone is considered to be of good enough character to pass the basic test, with some obvious exceptions relating mostly to criminal records.

The Firearms Act 1968 sets out who is prohibited from holding a certificate; we should note that where previous convictions are at issue, the sentence is the deciding factor, not what the sentence was for. However, section 21 of the Act allows one to appeal to the Crown Court (sitting in its capacity as successor to the Quarter Sessions) to have the prohibition lifted in light of the nature of your offence. One can, after all, find oneself banged up for all sorts of crimes that don't involve riot, recklessness or violence.

A three-year gaol term means that the person cannot possess firearms at any time after release without first obtaining leave of a Crown Court by way of an application. People in this position can't have airguns either, because these are firearms within the meaning of the Act, although exempt from the certificate system. They can, as it happens, still possess antiques, as nothing in the Act applies to them.

A sentence of more than three months, but less than three years, attracts a five-year prohibition starting from the day of release. The prohibition is determined by the sentence, not time served, so someone with a three-year stretch who serves one year and a day must still make an application to a court before taking possession of any firearm. Likewise, a sixteen-week sentence might entail only eight weeks inside, but the sentence was more than three months, so the five-year prohibition starts on the release date.

It is taken, from the word 'release' in the Act, that suspended sentences don't count towards this prohibition; a matter that the police have raised in connection with Derrick Bird. Adrian Whiting's report cites R *v. Fordham* (1969, in Kent) as the relevant decision. But Derrick Bird's suspended sentence was passed in 1990. So, even had section 21 prohibition applied to suspended sentences, he would still have been eligible to get ticket and his shotguns back 15 years before the murders. In his case, a 'tighter' law would have saved no lives.

People who are gaoled for offences that are not considered evidence of danger to public safety or the peace can—and do—apply to have the prohibition lifted early. In our experience, they're successful in most cases, if they leave their application long enough.

That is the basic model that dictates who should not have a certificate, and why and when. We know from various appeals heard in courts of record that non-violent offences and administrative firearms offences do not call for a certificate to be revoked, unless the penalty put the miscreant into the prohibited category.

How to be a danger to public safety and the (Queen's) peace

The Act has further tests of character to be considered. Whether a person poses a potential 'danger to public safety or the peace' is the key one, for all certificate holders and for dealers. The phrase is undefined in the Act, but has been the subject of judicial scrutiny from time to time, and there are published cases that the Home Office and the police could use for guidance—if only they would.

Some are straightforward enough and help to clarify the meaning of the Act. In *Ackers and others v Taylor* (1974, 1 All ER 771), Ackers and his friends were caught after poaching at night using legally-held shotguns. The court decided that using a legal gun for an illegal purpose breached the Queen's peace, and upheld the revocation of their certificates. Other cases smack of a try-on by the police and/or the Crown Prosecution Service (established 1986) in the hope of improving their statistics for successful prosecutions.

In *Spencer-Stewart v. Chief Constable of Kent* (*The Times*, 21 December 1988), the appellant had been convicted of deception, and the police warned him that another brush with them would result in revocation of his shotgun certificate. Mr Spencer-Stewart was nabbed next for handling stolen goods, and the police duly carried out their threat. The High Court found that Mr Spencer-Stewart's non-violent offence did not indicate that he was a 'danger to public safety or the peace'—the sole ground for revoking a shotgun certificate—and his appeal was allowed.

In the 1990s, Mr Edwards got into a violent domestic incident, which his local police used as grounds for revoking his shotgun certificate. On appeal (*Chief Constable of Norfolk v. Edwards* - CO 4442-96 and 1997 EWHC Admin 294) the High Court noted that while the incident was violent, it did not involve any guns. It could have, as Mr Edwards had access to them. That he did not resort to his weapons meant that he did not pose a danger to public safety or the peace; and thus he could have his certificate back.

Shepherd v. Chief constable of Devon and Cornwall (19 July 2002) is interesting because until Shepherd's case, the police always treated both firearm and shotgun certificates the same in revocations, so holders of both always lost both. Shepherd had hung on to his handguns after the 1997 ban and had lied to police about disposing of them. Having been found out (luckily for him before five-year sentences for possessing handguns became mandatory), he had both his certificates revoked. In the High Court, however, the judge decided that while concealing handguns and lying to police might be evidence that he was 'otherwise unfitted' to be entrusted with firearms, the firearms offence was non-violent, and no evidence of danger to public safety or the peace. So Mr Shepherd got his shotgun certificate back.

A long, complicated and expensive way to make a simple point

Essex police v. Germain on the other hand suggests that two drink-drive convictions within a 10-year period *is* evidence of being a danger to public safety or the peace. What that case actually highlights is the question of when a certificate is justifiably revoked, how long is it before the individual can restore his position?

The law allows you to apply at any time, so the cancellation of one certificate means just that. You could apply for a new one the next day. But while common sense says that would negate the sanction, there is no obvious guidance from the Home Office or the courts on this point. Germain got a three-year driving ban in 1990, which was a second conviction. The police revoked his shotgun certificate about six months later, and he appealed, successfully, to the Crown Court. The ever-cautious Essex police dug in their heels and appealed to the High Court. Citing a Scottish case (*Luke v. Little*), they argued that irresponsible use of a motor vehicle was analogous to irresponsible use of a shotgun. The High Court agreed.

Meanwhile, after two years of his driving ban, Germain had successfully applied to magistrates to be excused the rest of it. At this point he still had no shotgun certificate, which had been revoked on the strength of a motoring conviction—for which he'd now completed the penalty. By the time the case got to High Court, that ticket had expired. Germain put in a fresh application, which Essex police rejected, but indicated that he could have it reconsidered two years after getting his driving licence back—apparently unaware that he already did have it back. Naturally, Germain appealed. At the court door, he was told he would have his ticket back in three months.

The case was messy, and expensive for Essex ratepayers. And it highlights the kind of farce that can occur when unaccountable people venture into uncharted legal territory. The main effect of the case seems to be that if the police do revoke a certificate on the strength of a driving ban, the shooting ban lasts only as long as the driving one. How that makes the rest of us safer is anyone's guess.

The Germain case still leaves open the question of how long such an administrative ban should last, since there is no other guidance on the subject. Given the terms of prohibition under section 21 of the Act, logic suggests that any administrative ban should be for not more than five years (the life of a certificate).

What would remove the process from the whims of unaccountable bureaucrats and police, is a clear tariff—and an equally clear statement, either in law or in guidance, as to what should *and should not* be regarded as evidence of a risk of 'public danger'. Otherwise, we will continue to have what we have—bad practice, no one knowing quite where they stand, and the whole system sliding into disrepute.

CHAPTER TEN
KEEPING GUNS SAFE
—MAINLY FROM THE POLICE

T HE BASELINE for any system of issuing firearm and shotgun certificates is a character test that shows you're unlikely to misuse the weapons you own. There are two further matters to resolve—security, and firearms types. Security is at once both simple and complex. Simple, because we all understand the word and the principles behind it; complex, because the Firearms Act is silent on the subject.

As a prerequisite for owning firearms, security appears only in the Firearms Rules, which set out the templates for the various forms and certificates currently used. Both firearm and shotgun certificates include a condition to the effect that the guns held on the certificate have to be kept securely when not in use and, when removed from security for some purpose connected with their use, precautions should be taken to prevent access by unauthorized persons.

The condition is in two parts because of the way in which the Metropolitan Police, in particular, behaved in the 1980s. The 1969 Rules said that firearms had to be kept securely at all times when not in actual use. The Met decided that 'actual use' was being loaded and fired on a range. At all other times the firearm had to be in its secure place, whose details were noted on the firearm certificate. This meant that, in the Met's view, there wasn't a legal way short of magic or hyper-dimensional teleportation for the certificate holder ever to get a weapon to a range, a wood in Essex or a Scottish hill. And if he didn't use it, he'd lose it. There was one loophole for getting a gun to the range or elsewhere to shoot it: and that was scrupulously observing the Eleventh Commandment—"Thou shalt not get caught." But enough people were prosecuted for possessing their own property in places other than the range and their homes to bring the condition as it stood (and the Met, who had had so much make-work fun with it) into disrepute; and eventually it was amended, in 1988.

The Metropolitan Police's interpretation of a 'secure place' was what they'd inspected and approved. Firearms stolen from anywhere else resulted in their owner being prosecuted for failing to comply with the condition. Police have also enjoyed pushing this particular envelope by prosecuting people who'd had their locked and alarmed cars broken into, and their guns and ammunition stolen. Otherwise, it was difficult to argue that the security was adequate if some malefactor had breached it. That approach, combined with the alteration of the condition to reflect the need for firearms to be in transit, or otherwise in a lower standard of security, does make a good basis for 'best practice' base, albeit one that still gives the police frayed ends to try unpicking further.

If there's a problem, it's the police view that the condition is a 'one-size-fits-all' stipulation that applies to everyone throughout the country. It works reasonably well for target shooters, who take firearms from their security to a range or clay shoot and back again. It works less well for people travelling longer distances, such for deer stalking—particularly when the journey is on public transport, such as aircraft, when the firearm(s) pass into other hands. Technically, of course, airline officials are handling baggage, not guns, but responsibility for their security still apparently rests with the guns' owner, who has no control over them for much of the time.*

Another group who have problems with the condition (or rather, may find the police eyeing the chance of an easy conviction) are people who need to keep their guns handy all the time: the farm-hand or gamekeeper in his cottage, for example, where guns constantly need to be 'available for use'.

Let not the law stand in the way of the police

Although the police have no power to inspect security arrangements, and thus no mandate to spend public money on doing so, security checks are something that certificate holders have become used to. Security inspections have both positive and negative consequences. On the negative side, everyone knows that the police are making a record of where to look for our guns in the hope that one day they are ordered to collect them all up. We also know that police

---

* In passing, the amazing bureaucracy and costs of shipping inert ammunition components should not continue without some thorough overhaul of whatever regulations made that mess in the first place.

records of firearm security are not themselves always secure. For instance, in 1992 burglars broke into a certificate holder's home in Bolton and stole the safe containing his pistols—but left untouched an identical one next to it, containing only documents.

The positive side of these inspections has been that policemen have more experience than the rest of us in spotting weaknesses in security. Because they've all investigated burglaries, they know what keeps the bad guys out and what doesn't, so they are usually very good at giving advice on making the perimeters of your dwelling secure. Once indoors, we have a different view from the police of the way firearms should be protected from rogues and villains.

That's because we believe in concealment as a security tool. If the crook can't *find* it, he can't *steal* it—didn't the Dead Sea Scrolls remain safe in an unlocked cave for nearly 2000 years because they were so well concealed? The police prefer obvious hard-shell security, probably because it's easier for them to check. We think the final decision should rest with the owner, although not without getting advice and support. The *Dabek* case (see page 76) makes it clear that 'unauthorized persons' include members of your household who are not themselves certificate holders. So your security has to be proof against them, and take into account that they are already, and with your permission, inside the hard-shell security of your dwelling.

The essentials of good security

Basically, a good cabinet, concealed if possible, solidly fixed to the building, is what passes muster. Certificate holders should also beware that it's a bad idea to keep other valuables in with the guns. The gun cabinet should be for guns alone. By all means get a second safe to keep the ammunition in, but if you want somewhere for the wife's jewellery, it needs to be in security accessible to her—i.e., in her gun cabinet, not yours.

Sorting out security could be something your local crime prevention officer can help with, but we consider that your local firearms dealer, club secretary or independent security adviser (for instance, whoever installs the safe) could do just as well, and simultaneously save police time and taxpayers' money. In essence, what we say is that certificate holders should take adequate precautions, which are then checked independently by someone who certifies both the security and how many firearms can be held within it.

The police have made a shambles of this one, and in any case are acting *ultra vires*—beyond their legal powers—in faffing about at this level of detail. From time to time, too, their camouflage slips, and their political agenda becomes more obvious than usual. As when we had to go through the misery of their antics in 1991, when they heard a rumour that the British Standards Institute was going to issue a kitemark for gun cabinets. One force gleefully announced that all cabinets in their area would no longer meet approval, as they didn't have kitemarks. The BSI, to its credit, found a way around the minefield the Home Office had sown before them. So the police's next gambit was to pick an arbitrary number of guns and to publish advice to the effect that 'if you have more then 6/8/10/12/whatever, but take away the number you first thought, guns you may need an alarm to BSI 4737.'

Alarm systems work best on unoccupied premises. If the house is occupied in the daytime by your aging mother or a pet dog, the alarm system probably can't be set. And if it's set to cover only the area in which guns are stored, there is the greater risk of someone straying inadvertently into that area, or you setting it off by doing so since you didn't have to disarm the system at the front door.

And while we're at, why don't we fiddle the figures?

The bottom line is that gun-owners have invested money in valuable property and will naturally want to keep it secure—but not so secure that they can't get at it themselves when they want to. The Home Office studied the theft of firearms in 1991 and found that around 2000 guns a year were reportedly stolen. That figure was considerably higher than the number of guns that certificate holders reported as stolen to the certificate-issuing departments. It turned out that the figure was arrived at through 'tick-box' reporting by investigators. Those '2000 stolen guns' included glue-guns, hot-airguns, wall hangers, nail guns, airguns, toys—indeed anything that could be described by ticking the box marked 'gun' on the paperwork. As someone said at the time, if a few traffic cops had lost a few radar guns, that would have boosted the stats a bit further.

A more realistic figure seemed to be more like 400 guns stolen. Which is a lot of metal, but as a proportion of weapons held in private houses, it's a tiny fraction. What was even more interesting in the Home Office study was *how* those guns were stolen. More than a third of them went missing because burglars either opened the cabinet, typically by finding the spare keys, or ripped the whole cabinet off the wall and made off with it. While Home Office advice to certificate holders has been updated since this research was published, the advice has not been modified to highlight these weaknesses.

Neither of these larcenous methods would work if the cabinet (or just the guns) were sufficiently well-hidden to prevent the burglar finding them in the first place. Consider your own security and think about the Gestapo searching for evidence that you're a *résistant*. If they find the evidence, you're in trouble, so effective concealment is essential. It's no different today—if a gun cabinet is necessary, professional installation should be considered to make sure it stays attached to the building; and it needs to be thoroughly masked afterwards. Don't keep spare keys at home; they could be kept at your brother's or with another certificate holder, but not on the premises. The person holding spare keys for you has no access to your guns, because the hard shell security of your dwelling is in his way.

The end play for security is a certificate of adequacy issued by a competent inspecting authority or installation company, stating the number of guns that can be effectively stored in it: your security provider could do that as part of their service package. That would free up police resources for other priorities. Your club could provide this service also, since its officials know at least as much as any other authority the best way to store firearms securely.

CHAPTER ELEVEN
PUBLIC SAFETY MEANS SHOOTING SAFELY

P UBLIC SAFETY really has two aspects, when it comes to firearms. First, there's the delicate matter of the shooter's character. In practice this means that some members of the public,
who happen to be civil servants, deem other members of the public
insufficiently fragrant to be allowed entrance to the guild of firearms
owners. The other aspect of public safety, and the more real one, is
knowing how and when using a firearm can go sufficiently wrong to
put other people in real danger—and knowing how to avoid that.

Let's take that second aspect first. Every firearm is by definition
capable of launching a projectile, and while it's moving that projectile
is capable of harming, to some degree, anyone who gets in its way. So
to avoid such missiles when they're flying about, all you have to do is
stay out of harm's way. That means not walking your dog on a military range during firing times, and not driving your jet-ski between
the red flags marking the danger area of an on-shore range.

You could also consider staying off private property. In July 2009
a gaggle of Norwegian tourists moseyed into a Wiltshire field to take
a gander at a 300ft-wide crop circle imprinted there. Any hopes they
may have entertained of enjoying a mystical experience or two were
promptly shattered by several blasts from a shotgun. The New-Age
Norwegians thought they were being shot at—which may indicate
that they were aware they were trespassing. "It was totally unnecessary and incredibly scary," grumbled 47-year-old Eva-Marie Brekkes-
bo (whose name suggests she may be a cereal-killer herself). A mobile
phone was urgently deployed, and ere long Wiltshire's finest's heli-
copter thwacked into view, as did a vanload of black-clad Plods toting submachine guns. As it turned out, the 'gunman', one Kenneth
Wilson, had been lurking amid the (not so alien) corn, and had been

shooting at pigeons, with the standing permission of the landowner, farmer Richard Oram. No charges were brought, which was satisfying for Mr Wilson. (The incident was no doubt equally satisfying for Wiltshire's tactical firearms team, whose existence and large budget it had helped to justify, in their minds at least.) The fact remains that the Norwegians were where they should not have been, whereas Mr Wilson was not.

So, don't wander about on private land without permission. Anyone shooting on it has no reason to expect you to be there, and the consequences could be both fatal and your own silly fault.

Those are, really, all precautions the non-shooting, fresh-air-breathing public need take. The rest of it is up to shooters, who have an obligation not to let their fast-flying lead stray into areas where people are entitled to be, lest that lead stray inside people themselves.

Indoors or outdoors with a gun, stay safe

We can divide shooters into three classes for this; first, there are members of shooting clubs, shooting on ranges. Indoor ranges are self-contained, so no ammunition should escape from them. If it does, there's a fault in construction or maintenance to deal with. Outdoor ranges come in two main types—'danger area' ranges and 'no danger area' ranges. The first type are mostly military. Pirbright and Bisley ranges have a danger area that is common land, to which the public have the right of access outside of shooting times. Within the shooting periods, it would be dangerous to enter. Proving the point, on a saunter there at a safe time you won't take long to find spent bullets on the ground.

When using such a range, the shooter can't see the danger area, so responsibility for safety rests with the public, who should note the red flags flying and not stray into the gunfire. On a 'no danger area' range, the shooter can see the backstop and thus any people or sheep or horses straying onto it. Such ranges are also usually marked by red flags and are usually private property, so strolling into harm's way is stupid, in the case of sheep, or intentionally disruptive and/or stupid in the case of people. Either way, safety is the shooters' responsibility—but, as they can see who or what's in jeopardy, they can do something about it before letting a shot break. We have seen opinion divided on this point only once, when three metres' worth of feral python slid elegantly across the butts on an outdoor pistol range.

Next up are field shooters, who generally don't use firearms on ranges, except to zero them. They carry rifles for deer stalking, shotguns and smaller calibre rifles for pest control, and airguns for smaller pests; they use shotguns at clay pigeon shoots, or when rough shooting or on driven game shoots; and airguns when target shooting on private property. It is up to all these people to know the capability of their guns and not to take a shot that could—no matter how remote the chance—harm people, livestock, or protected wildlife. This is why training and mentoring are so important in keeping field sports safe.

Mr Plod would like to see your fields. And you, too

Naturally, the police, spying new opportunities to meddle and snoop and push forward the bounds of empire, have decided to see all this a little differently. When firearms require a certificate, the police have been involved in 'land inspection' for the last quarter-century or so, ostensibly to raise public safety issues, if they can find any. Actually, this is just a cover story. The origin of 'land inspection' was so that a police force in one part of the country, such as Manchester, had a job-justifying reason to notify a police force in another part of the country, such as Devon, that so-and-so had applied for a certificate to use a rifle on a named farm or estate.

Any local police objections to the suitability of the land (which may put the grant of a certificate in jeopardy) will then be made to the force to which the application was originally made. Such objections have included proximity of roads and footpaths, caravan sites, a lack of the declared target species—and even the character of the landowner; but perhaps he was an 'intellectual malcontent', with a quixotic yen for individual liberty and an automatic pistol.

People who apply to use a registered rifle on land are divided by police policy (not knowledge) into beginners and experienced. Beginners usually get a certificate naming the piece of land, but with permission extending to any other land 'deemed suitable' by the police. Previous experience on ranges or as a teenager with a shotgun under Dad's supervision and advice doesn't count, because the police are careful not to ask about anything so relevant. Experienced shooters, usually defined as such at first renewal, get an 'open certificate'; this sometimes names the principal location, but extends to any other land over which the certificate holder has got permission to shoot.

This bit of empire-building *can* be seen as having some useful purpose, in that some land may turn out to be too small for the intended ammunition, in the opinion of the—usually unqualified and inexperienced—person inspecting it. Whatever is being used, the ammunition mustn't stray beyond the land's borders. Most parcels of land in the UK are too small to catch a .308/7.62 bullet if it's fired upward at an angle of about 30 degrees or more. But what makes the real difference to where the bullet goes is the person firing it. This is something the police seem incapable of absorbing. Just as they come over all shaky at the thought of people owning examples of inert precision engineering, *alias* guns, they seem to think that *where* a person shoots will supernaturally affect their skill, judgement, and common sense.

Good old stalkers beget good young stalkers

Careless habits (or even thoughts) with guns are a matter for training, and people who take random shots at unsafe angles are very soon caught by coaches; and they're soon broken of the tendency or encouraged to take up another hobby, such as collecting horse brasses. Most people who stalk deer either learned the art from a mentor—their Dad, a gamekeeper, a favourite uncle; or they may have gone on a formal course with a shooting organization, or an informal one, by booking a 'stalking experience' on an estate and using the estate rifle. That gets you the undivided attention of an estate gamekeeper or ghillie, and the benefit of a lifetime's wisdom, skill and experience. This too the police find hard to digest. Could it be that they just don't trust us?

The basics of shooting deer are first to identify the target correctly and *at the same time* to see it in the context of a safe backstop. We say 'correct' target because deer come in all ages and two sexes and, depending on the time of year, only the male or the female is fair game—never both at the same time. So the stalker has to identify his deer as one he can legally shoot on the day he's looking at it. The backstop question is common to both stags and does, and to all rifle shooting in the field. The question you must answer is this: when you look at a deer through your telescopic sight, is there something behind it that will stop your bullet once it's gone through the deer?

You must see target and backstop—solid ground, visibly within range of your ammunition—as a *complete* sight picture. As a rule of thumb, if you can see sky in your telescopic sight, it's probably not a safe shot. The same applies to shooting a fox with a .22WMR. That unmissable skyline silhouette may be ever so tempting one day, and that hedge behind him seems really, really thick on another. Don't take the shot. But, whatever the circumstances, the final decision is that of the person with his finger on the trigger. At that point it doesn't matter what the police thought of the land or its owner. Safety is the shooter's province.

It is rather easier to get the certificate for smaller calibre rifles and shotguns without any training. It's possible to become a landowner and apply for the appropriate certificates to deal with that noisy rookery, rat infestation or smelly fox without much input from anyone else. The police may well hone your initial choice of rifle as part of the application process, not necessarily helpfully. Because of, and for the sake of, bureaucratic tidiness, Home Office guidance has a list of calibres in it together with what the Home Office thinks they're suitable for. How they come to the conclusions they do is something of an unexplained phenomenon, not unlike poltergeists and UFOs.

You can look up the details for yourself, of course. But in simple terms, the Home Office has decided—by scrutinizing the entrails of pigeons?—that ammunition powerful enough for deer, as defined by the Deer Act, is *too* powerful for smaller species. We would observe, not from a desk but from some decades' experience with all manner of firearms, that some foxes are bigger than some deer. And a safe shot at a fox with a .22 rifle is also a safe shot with one taking .600 Nitro Express; and besides, the fox is more certainly dead when shot with the latter than with the former. The .600 will likely make a rabbit inedible, it's true, but there are plenty of calibres that are capable of a head shot on that greedy little fast-breeder, and not all of them are smaller than the minimum legal calibre for deer. In England and Wales, that is .240, so anything smaller than that is—officially—more suitable for foxes and rabbits and such.*

It's a matter of trust. And they don't trust any of us

If all that sounds odd, bordering on the weird, remember that all these criteria have been dreamt up to protect their creators' jobs and pensions, and have nothing to do with public safety, let alone animal welfare. If our previously-mentioned London escapee is not a club shooter and has no mentor to hand, his best access to advice will be his neighbours or his firearms dealer.

And what a can of worms that opens for discussion!

Basically, the Home Office has no faith either in the gun trade or in the members of its own officially-approved network of rifle and pistol clubs. The problem with both, in what passes for a mind in bureaucratic circles, is that dealers and club secretaries would rather like to promote the shooting sports and recruit new people to them.

---

* The Home Office has also plucked out of thin air an arbitrary *maximum* power for ammunition to use on deer, so some traditional deer cartridges are now 'too powerful' for bureaucratic comfort, and will only be authorized for big game abroad. And (extra cream for the cake) because these calibres are *so* dangerous, you can't practise with them in the UK either. Isn't the country big enough? Is it bereft of rifle ranges?

Presumably other organizations and networks like the Automobile Association, the local bowling club and the Rotarians don't. To see the shooting sports expand is contrary to policy. Exactly *whose* policy that is, is not clear, but we know it's contrary to the Police Federation's wish-list, while the Labour government of 1997–2010 certainly made its anti-gun position very clear.

That government did not make it illegal to join or promote shooting sports, although police did object to certain dealerships and some individuals on the grounds that their activities were promoting shooting or likely to increase the number of certificates on issue in their area, as if it were an offence to do so. The government needs to get off the fence—in other words, get its employees under control—on this particular subject. Then we will all know where they, and we, stand. If it's to be government policy that the shooting sports may decline, but not grow, they should put that into legislation—and then see what we do about their violation of our constitution.

If on the other hand their policy is to act lawfully, then they should, at very least, get their unnecessary public servants to comply with the legislation as it stands.

When deliberate ignorance is unalloyed bliss

That's the background as we see it. In essence the problem is that bureaucrats see firearms dealers and club officials as self-serving. They think that dealers lack all sense of self-preservation, and will try to bring unsuitable people into the shooting sports just to get the additional sales, while club officials want to inflate their own empires (wonder where they got that idea?). And so, dealers are not trusted to counter-sign certificate applications. But firearms dealers are businessmen; they come into retailing firearms from a variety of backgrounds and are not necessarily experts in all or, indeed, in any shooting disciplines. They are, however, focal points in their communities. It would not take a dealership long to identify those experts in their neighbourhood who could serve as consultants for specific matters. But that's not how they are treated.

Club officials similarly enjoy little credibility when the police are making decisions about who or who should not hold a certificate, and the idea that they, *especially*, may want to keep dodgy characters out of their sport crosses the mind of no one with real power. The Home Office prefers applicants to have two referees who are *not* shooters to help the police decide who should have a certificate. This is rather like seeking advice from deep-sea divers as to who should be trusted to fly an aeroplane. Presumably the Home Office and police think this is what constitutes an objective and disinterested opinion.

So: the people who actually serve the shooting sports are not deemed trustworthy when it comes to deciding who else should be allowed to join them; and thus the police are left to make decisions on their own. The case of Derrick Bird shows where this gets you. He wasn't in a shooting club, and his local dealers didn't know him: so there probably wasn't anyone, apart from him, with whom the police could have discussed his applications. ACC Adrian Whiting assures us that everything was done by the book. We don't doubt it. The trouble is that the book was written by idiots. These people couldn't recognize a potential intelligence network if it announced itself with a fanfare and, bare-naked, did cartwheels down Whitehall.

There is another way of doing things

It is actually unnecessary for a responsible official, signing approvals for firearms certificates, to have local knowledge—*provided* the right information has already been collected at ground level. Our notional alternative to the present mess has three stages, and they're inexpensive and intelligence-led to boot.

First, a fit person certificate, which is essentially a criminal records check, obtained by the issuing authority and copied to the applicant, as happens with applications to the Security Industry Authority. The next requirement is a security inspection certificate, also from a competent authority, such as the installer, or a club official. What firearms are suitable to the applicant is for the applicant and his club secretary to decide or, for those not in target-shooting clubs, his dealership and his mentor. In either case the applicant should be regarded—'signed off'—as competent to use safely the guns he wants to own. Whoever does the signing-off doesn't need another set of bureaucratic hoops to jump through to qualify as competent himself. A couple of references from equally knowledgeable people should be sufficient.

The current government's hope is that the community will take on things we currently pay public servants to do. Here's a fine opportunity to show how it could work. There are a few other areas of shooting that could also do with being freed from the sticky tentacles of bureaucracy, so we'll tackle those next.

For example. The Home Office currently insists that new members of shooting clubs serve a probation period; we say that they should train with the club for as long as it takes, be it a month or be it a year, to be awarded a certificate of competence for the type of firearms they wish to acquire on their own certificate. Teaching the basics is fundamental to what clubs do but, to make progress, a tyro has to obtain his own firearms if he's to develop—just as he does with a motor vehicle or a musical instrument. The school car or flute only gets you so far. Armed with their own kit, along with some experience and expert advice, newcomers can then take best advantage of what clubs also do—bring in coaches from county level or sports psychologists from the national organizations—to refine their techniques or purge themselves of bad habits.

The probation period as we know it is really a bureaucratic one-size-fits-all wheeze, or obstacle, designed to handle a problem that doesn't really exist. Whereas (paradoxically) the concept of a certificate of competence is already well-understood by civil servants. What we're proposing is essentially the same as a driving test: you get the basic document (a provisional licence) and take that to a school, take lessons, pass a test that's uniform throughout the land, and get a certificate of competence. Driving courses vary: getting through the test in a car or on a motorbike—a lethal device if there ever was—typically takes from a dozen to 20 hours' tuition. Shooting is about the same to begin with.

Training makes you safe. The law should encourage it

Advanced driving courses, such as for large goods vehicles, tend to be consolidated courses, taking several hours a day over several days with a test at the end. Typically, 16 hours of training fits you to drive a heavy goods vehicle. A shooter with one discipline and one type of gun, like a driver of one vehicle type, has already had to master all the basic rules and techniques, most of which are common to every kind of firearm or vehicle.

Building on that demands training in the specifics of a new weapon and the disciplines that go with it. At the end of a course that, say, teaches already-competent rifle shooters to use .22 pistols safely (which includes accurately), the student will take a test to demonstrate his grasp of safe gun-handling, range manners and commands, and shooting theory; and will need to achieve a minimum standard in shooting (UIT Standard Pistol comes to mind as a good all-round test), with both revolvers and semi-autos, to be deemed competent.

A shooter graduating from .22 pistol to fullbore pistol should still have to demonstrate that he's safe and polite on the range, but the core test of competence will lie in his gun-handling and accuracy. An acceptable score in some variation on the NPA Police Pistol I course of fire suggests itself as appropriate for this transition.

Every firearm and shotgun certificate should include a condition authorizing the certificate holder to teach other people by allowing them to use his guns while under his immediate control. The 1988 Act already makes that legal for rifle owners; the 1968 Act makes it legal in certain circumstances for shotgun owners, but the law is confusing because of its ambiguous wording. At the moment, you can, without holding a certificate, borrow a shotgun from the 'occupier' of private premises and use it on those premises in his presence. The flaw is the word 'occupier'.

Naturally (inevitably—sigh) police have tried prosecuting shotgun certificate holders where they are, say the police, not 'occupiers' in the sense of owners, but merely have permission to be on a particular bit of land. It's an easy arrest for a victimless offence—just the kind our police love—and is doubtless on Prof. Peter Squires's list of 55 naughty things you can do with guns without even having to think about it. That kind of nonsense is easily remedied, by issuing unambiguous guidance. There should also be a condition—or more accurately a permission—on certificates to encourage mentoring. Under 1968 rules, one could borrow any firearm at an approved club and use it with the owner's permission and in his presence. That needs to be restored, and one should be able to do the same with shotguns, wherever the owner has permission to shoot. The more training, formal and informal, is encouraged, the greater the safety of the sport.

The problem with airguns is not with airguns

The other category of firearm whose misuse endangers public safety from time to time is low-powered airguns. These probably feature more in the news when involved in mischief than any type of firearm on certificate, and they certainly feature in political thinking quite often. Low-powered airguns, as defined in law, are rifles that have a striking energy of less than 12ft/lb, and pistols that produce less than 6 ft/lb. Twelve ft/lb is sufficient to crack 3mm-thick window glass, but not the 4mm glass that has been the minimum thickness in double glazing for about 20 years. Remember the old two-ounce tobacco tin that everyone used to keep spare nails and screws in? An air rifle under the 12 ft/lb limit will penetrate one skin and bend the other. Over the limit, and the pellet will make a complete hole through both sides. This is rule of thumb—don't use it as expert evidence in court.

If a typical air rifle sold in the UK does about 10.5 foot/pounds after some wear and tear, it's still producing more than enough energy to put a pellet straight through your spectacles and destroy your eye and possibly your brain. So it's not a toy. Air pistol pellets likewise will go straight through spectacles and eyeballs, and must be used properly and treated with respect. They are exempt from the need to hold a certificate for them and, despite age restrictions, so many households have them that young people do get to play with them from time to time.

The problem, in our view, falls into two parts. First, there are very few places that are set up to let people walk in off the street, learn to use airguns safely, and practise with them. People buying a cartridge rifle, or a shotgun, don't expect to use it at home, unless their house sits on a chunk of land. To be used, the gun goes to the club range, the clay shoot—it goes somewhere safe to use it. Airgunners don't have the same option. A lot of ranges that could once have given them houseroom now cannot because the Home Office abolished day membership of approved clubs—and in any case most have closed since the handgun ban.

Local authorities could, but don't, provide facilities for shooting in the way they do for swimming—although that's a more dangerous activity, with way more fatalities every year than in shooting. There's also no current system through which people could find out how to make a safe range at home for their friends and children to use; that's something else local authorities could supply. It's not that difficult to set up a safe range facility for low-powered airguns. It does takes some competence—somebody who knows what to think about, how to train beginners, and how to catch the pellets effectively. Local shooting clubs could, and surely would, help out here.

Ignorance is not so blissful

The second part of the problem is that young people, in particular, get access to airguns and use them without knowing basic safe gun-handling, and without understanding the ballistics of the ammunition. So cats and children get shot and (old) windows get broken. Politicians tend to perceive the gun as the problem, rather than seeing the social cause behind the injuries and the damage. And politicians' 'solutions' tend be restrictive—they think that by raising the age limit, or banning something, they will somehow make a difference.

We think they won't. But they could go a very long way toward solving the problem by providing easily-accessible facilities where people can be taught how to do things safely. Swimming is widely taught; there are pools in most communities. The result is that fatal accidents usually involve the unwise swimming in unsafe places. If you close swimming pools and restrict legal swimming to those over 18, your legislation will have a dramatic impact on the accident rate—people will drown using *ad hoc* ponds, canals and the seaside. You certainly won't have made Britain any safer. It's not clever to think that such an approach will work for airguns.

Creating facilities where your safety has been planned for and where instruction is available is a far wiser policy. The result will be that fewer airguns will be used ignorantly and dangerously, causing damage and injury. Naturally, we don't expect politicians to like this idea. It's altogether too positive—trusting and encouraging people to improve their behaviour, rather than smacking the naughty. Politicians naturally favour restrictions: passing a law that stops (or that pretends to stop) people doing something is a bracing exercise of power, after all. Similarly, the police won't be keen on airgun owners taking weapons through public places to get to a safe place to use them. Both sets of distrustful obsessive-compulsives should seek medication or therapy.

Hot air, inconvenience, and expense descend on Scotland

We should mention in passing the appearance in Scotland of what could turn out to be the thin end of a particularly nasty, pointless, and expensive wedge. In December 2010 one Jennifer Pasquill, the senior pen-pusher at the Police Division of the Scottish government's Safer Communities Directorate (*sic*), explained what would happen once the power to 'regulate' airguns was devolved to Scotland:

> Upon the powers being transferred, it is likely that a pilot licensing scheme for air weapons will be set up. This will enable us to test the practicalities of air weapon licensing. It will also test whether or not a licensing system can operate effectively without wider reform of the firearms legislation. If a pilot is commissioned, the scheme take place [*sic*] in one or more areas in Scotland and will be evaluated.

Translation: we will set up a pilot licensing scheme in the hope that it will prove a bit awkward, or expensive, for everyone because it's not integrated into the certification system. Then we will have an excuse to try to persuade the Westminster government to devolve all firearms regulation in Scotland to us. And don't think the word 'evaluated' is there to suggest we'll drop airgun licensing should the pilot scheme turn out to show that the whole idea is a waste of time. And then once we've made a hash of it in Scotland, Westminster will dump it on England and Wales. Ms Pasquill further passed her quill:

> To oversee the pilot and to aid broader consideration of air weapons and firearms issues we will establish a Scottish Firearms Consultative Panel. A broad spectrum of interests will be represented on the Panel, which will include those who attended the Firearms Summit we held in May

2008 as well as those who were involved in the development of our firearms public information campaign last year. Interests invited to attend Panel meetings will include the Association of Chief Police Officers in Scotland, the Convention of Scottish Local Authorities, the Scottish Target Shooting Federation, the Gun Control Network and the British Association for Shooting and Conservation.

Translation: we will set up a talking shop at great public expense; incidentally it will feature many excellent opportunities for its members to make exorbitant expenses claims, and it will include a number of unrepresentative professional gun-grabbers, who by chance will outnumber those with any useful knowledge of the subject by three to two. You can take it as read that a 'Scottish Firearms Consultative Panel' will not limit its disquisitions to airguns. Folk like us can smell an empire-building opportunity before it comes over the horizon.

> While our primary concern is for public safety, we are clear that any licensing system must be workable for the police and all involved. The Scottish Government will work closely with the Consultative Panel to ensure this is the case.

Translation: whatever happens, ye puir wee bairns, we'll find a way to shove this one through.

How whatever new procedure the jobsworths dream up will actually improve public safety is left unexplained: it's just taken for granted that magically it will. We beg leave to doubt that. The new licensing system—and we suspect it *will* be that, not one of certification and registration—will initially apply only to sales of new airguns. That will leave approximately 580,000 airguns already in Scotland unlicensed (or unregistered) and beyond the reach of the authorities—for the time being, at least. So, once again, where's the advantage?

And if, in due course, all airgun owners in Scotland are required to register their weapons, the authors of this book will, within two years of such a law being enacted, faithfully observe the following schedule of donations to a charity of their choice:
- For a take-up of more than 12,000 (2+ percent)—£25
- For a take-up of more than 60,000 (10+ percent)—£100
- For a take-up of more than 300,000 (50+ percent)—£1000.

CHAPTER TWELVE
REDUCE RED TAPE, EXPAND THE ECONOMY

B Y NOW THE READER should have a pretty clear idea of our proposals for simplifying and streamlining the issue of firearm certificates—and, thereby, reducing the cost of the system to the public purse, and possibly even making it of some benefit to public safety. It boils down to requiring anyone who wants to own guns and shoot them to obtain a fit person certificate, validation of their security arrangements, and certificates of competence for each type of firearm sought. The complete document should be issued by an *accountable* national body—of which more in the next chapter.

The next step is to inject some sanity, simplicity and logic into the firearms trade. Our view is that firearms dealers should be hooked up to national database, so that when they sell you something, the transaction is recorded on-line, instantly transferring the firearm from his stock to your certificate, in a corollary of the other part of the deal, in which the money shifts from your account to his.

We don't know to what extent a national database would be worth the cost of setting it up, but it would have to be inclusive. At the moment, the evidence suggests, the vast majority of firearms in the UK are unregistered. Most, we suspect, are sleepers, gathering dust in cupboards and drawers, but there are a good number of rifles in clubs and galleries that do not have to be registered at the moment. None of the police's and security services' firearms are registered; nor are military stocks. It's illogical to have them outside the system, as they're just as vulnerable to misuse or theft as those in private hands.

Let's see how our system will work in practice.

When a firearm is registered on the national database for the first time, it generates a computer file, which becomes that weapon's virtual identity throughout its career. In order to reduce the unregistered pool, it should be possible for any owner, inheritor or executor to register firearms at any time. This creates the computer file, and registration alone is that person's authority for continued possession while they sort out what to do next: whether to go through the necessary processes to become keepers (no ammunition), or shooters (with ammunition), or whether to dispose of the gun(s) through the trade or at auction. Some estates can take forever to go through probate, so there has to be flexibility (perhaps a system of extensions of authority on well-defined 'reasonable grounds') built in to the way heirlooms are handled.

Ammunition purchases are likewise fired straight into the database, so that anomalous transactions stand out, and can be flagged up as possibly worthy of investigation. Thomas Hamilton, for example, was dormant as a shooter for a long period, but then he suddenly bought a lot of ammunition—2300 rounds in a five-month period, after eight years without buying any at all. A nationwide computerized system would have logged the status of his club membership (expired) and flagged up his sudden resurrection of interest despite his apparently having nowhere to shoot. Computer systems were capable of spotting this kind of anomalous spike in traffic in the 1970s, so we're not exactly asking for digital miracles here.

Now take the guns held by the police and the military. Most firearms used by police are imports. Somebody brings them into the UK on an import licence and, the way we'd have it, registers them on the national database when they arrive. When collected by a police force, the database entry is amended to show who's got them; and when they return to the trade—police firearms are traded in, old for new, periodically—the database is amended again. Likewise, military small arms go onto the database as they roll off the UK production line or when they come into the country, and are booked out to units or unit armouries, and to individual soldiers, as they're issued.

Existing police and military stocks should also go on the database, which would give useful if temporary work to those clerks about to become redundant in the wake of our other reforms.

Business is business; times are hard. So give gunshops a break

First, a quick survey of the way things are. Firearms dealers are registered by their local police, in fact separately by every local police force in whose area the dealer has trading premises. These premises can be temporary, such as for country fairs, or permanent trading positions in a retail shop, factory, warehouse, clubhouse—anywhere that sales take place. A dealer so registered can buy (but not sell) anywhere; he does not need to be on his own premises, or anybody else's for that matter, or in his own police area. He could be at a country house auction, in a deceased person's former abode, someone else's shop, in a car park or layby. It's the place where firearms are exposed for sale that has to be registered, and sales have to be 'in person': the buyer has to attend the registered premises to complete the transaction. A dealership can be an individual, partnership or company. What it takes to get registered is good character, suitable premises and a business plan.

The 1988 Act amended the law giving the police discretion to refuse to register anyone who did not appear to them to be intent on trading to a substantial extent, except as part of another trade, business or profession. So there are three criteria in play—the character of the applicant, the adequacy of his premises, and then the question of whether the dealership is to be a small but necessary part of a larger business (such as a jobbing journalist who also reviews guns, or a company supplying props to the film industry, or a magazine photographer), or a substantial business in its own right. As far as we know this is the only instance in British law of the police being appointed judges, and not very accountable ones at that, of someone's entrepreneurial potential.

Dealers who aren't dealers

The reason for the 1988 amendment was that some police forces had used dealer registration as a solution to problems arising from frequent firearms transactions; mainly collectors, who were frowned upon by McKay in 1972. For people collecting firearms or changing firearms frequently—a term that can have as many meanings as there are police forces—a dealer's registration saved a lot of unnecessary paper-shuffling. In the course of the 1988 bill's passage the government accepted that there were people who had to be registered as dealers but did not actively trade in guns as such.

Other examples included a patent agent, who might never have a gun in his possession unless an inventor walks in with one for him to work from. There are also people on the periphery of the gun trade who will have guns go through their hands without trading (in guns) to any substantial extent. A stock maker, for example, might never sell a gun in his life, but there's always one on the bench being fitted with new woodwork. The same is true for other customization work: component-part manufacturers may well need a sealed pattern sample against which to check their work, as might a holster-maker, but neither will buy or sell any guns.

A lot of these people are in business before the question of having to register as a 'firearms dealer' arises. All they really need, to do what they do, is a fit-person certificate, and adequate storage. That should be noted on a certificate issued by a national body with consistent criteria and adequate accountability. The police really need have nothing to do with it.

Making it up as they go along

The unhelpful way the police handle non-dealing 'dealers' is a tiny problem compared with the way they manage actual firearms dealers. A chief constable regulates the conduct of officers on his own force and is also, it seems, responsible for regulating the firearms dealers in his area. No chief officer in the land applies the same standards to both; the gun trade report a huge number of difficulties, many of them quite simple to resolve, but caused because the police—not being businessmen—have either no guidance, or inconsistent guidance on how to manage the gun trade. And when in doubt (and often when not), they just make up the law as they go along.

For instance. The Firearms Rules lay down the format for dealers' registers. The register should be in four parts, which could be separate books. Part 1 lists guns manufactured, the entry showing the date of completion. Part 2 lists 'guns in' by date. Part 3 lists 'guns out'—*by date*. Part 4 is an inventory of guns on premises at a given date.

Part 4 is used only once a business has been running. In effect, one might take an annual inventory into a Part 4 register, then start new parts 1, 2 and 3. Simple, or what? But we have yet to meet a police officer who's familiar with this government-prescribed, statutory system. We've met a lot of policemen who want registers kept in Poor-Law hospital style—'guns in' on the left page and an entry opposite for 'guns out'. The trouble is, it's (a) not legal and (b) no help to the business. Booking guns in is not so bad: 50 guns from an auction just need to be listed. It's in booking them out that the police create a problem here: the Part 3 entries will not be in date order, bound as they would be in that system to be opposite the 'in' entry.

The Home Office struggled for years to avoid recognizing computer registers as legally compliant, without ever managing to put the police straight about the law on manual registers. As most policemen dealing with the trade are looking for an opportunity to prosecute, they rarely (never, in our experience) offer help in coping with any of the problematic transactions that a dealer may have to articulate into his records. Such as the old shotgun left on the back doorstep; there are all manner of variations on the theme of the anonymous hand-in.

A perennial issue is recording the status of guns that leave the dealer's premises temporarily, without being sold. They might pass to a journalist for review, to a repairman or stocker, to another dealer when storage space is tight, or on sale-or-return. They might go with him to another trading premises, such as at a game fair. A Part 3 'guns out' entry is inappropriate, and the Firearms Rules are silent on the subject. So a dealer isn't *legally* obliged to keep a record, although he'll want to make notes of his own, to keep track of stock.

If a chief constable had to keep a similar register of all the vehicles in his fleet, would he make a Part 3 entry when a vehicle went out on patrol? And to whom would he book it out? He doesn't and he wouldn't, of course, but he won't apply that logic to a firearms dealer's business. Custom and practice in the trade is to keep a separate record of such movements, to keep track of the valuable property involved; some police forces accept such actions, others see it as an opportunity to close the business.

Stuff that falls between the cracks

There are numerous transactions that have a straightforward format, but Home Office guidance to the police is silent—that is, useless—about them. Most involve firearms and shotguns passing between certificate holders, or *via* a dealer. Sleepers turn up from time to time; stuff left in cupboards and drawers until a death in the family prompts a clearout. They have to enter a dealer's register as coming from someone—the deceased, ideally, as then some nit-picking pedant can't prosecute them retrospectively for illegal possession.

Things get more complicated when a certificate holder goes overseas and acquires something he has authority to buy in the UK. The foreign dealer should not enter it on the certificate; if he does, he's unlikely to send the correct notice to the issuing authorities—who don't always put their address on the tickets they issue, you know. What the new owner should do is declare the piece to Customs in the red channel as he enters the UK and then, within a week, he should send his certificate to his chief constable with a note to say what he has acquired. The police bureaucracy can then delete the 'authority to acquire' and substitute 'authority to possess'.

What about antiques? The Act says that nothing in it applies to antique firearms kept solely as a curiosity or ornament, so they're off ticket. But dealers don't keep them as curiosities or ornaments—they keep them as stock. So would you, if wearing a pointy helmet, expect the dealer to have his antique Snider rifles in his register? The answer is not to be found in Home Office guidance. That leaves you, hiding under your helmet, the choice of exercising some pragmatic common sense, or creating a choice bit of aggravation.

Since too much clarity would reduce police scope for harassment, specious prosecutions, and inventing their own law, the guidance remains vague, silent, or unhelpful on these issues and many another. Incomplete, at best. Common sense, which the Home Office may (in our dreams) have hoped would fill the gap in their guidance, doesn't have anything to do with what happens on the ground. Nor does consistency from one police force to another. The relationship between the gun trade and the police has become so poor that it would be far better to have a new, national regulatory body overseeing dealer registrations. That body should also maintain a national database so that firearms dealers upload their transactions to the database as they happen instead of keeping a paper register on their premises.

The police would then be free to inspect the dealer's transaction records from the comfort of their own offices and free to investigate suspect transactions, without it being their responsibility (or caprice) to decide whether the business can continue trading or not. So many dealerships have been shut down arbitrarily by local police that one has to conclude they have actively been seeking excuses, no matter how slim, to do so. Too many to mention here, but in almost every case the police's rationale has involved their interpretation of record-keeping or a suspect transaction. And that (see below) is not lawful.

The record keeping, we repeat, should be a national affair. Dealers will want, and indeed need, to keep records for their accountant, their tax and VAT returns, their business development analyst, their own peace of mind.

The unreadable rifle: a Farsi farce from the inscrutable Orient

What constitutes a suspect transaction needs to be clarified by government, if it's in the public interest—which seems likely, given the absence of common sense in this area, and the rarity of cases that involve actually dishonest intent. For an instance of the kind of Keystone-level antics that flourish under the current régime, consider the following true story of a Persian-contract Mauser rifle. This is the same as the Great War German rifle, except that it was made for the Persian army. So the serial number is in Farsi. What should the dealer put in his register?

A London auctioneer sold this Persian Mauser as having 'no visible number' to a dealer, who had the wit to translate the Farsi into Arabic numbers (the ones we use) to put in his register. As did the dealer he sold it to. That dealer put it on a Lancashire firearm certificate. In those days, Lancashire had a cost-efficient (not) policy of sending two uniforms round to any firearm-certificate holder who'd recently bought something, just to check that the transaction was all above board, that the firearm complied with the legislation, and so forth (Parkinson's law in action: work expands to fill available time). In this case, they had the entry on the firearm certificate, but couldn't find the serial number mentioned on the rifle. Their training did not extend to the thought that Persian weapons might have Farsi numbers, or Russian ones numbers in Cyrillic, or that Smith and Wesson revolvers have serial numbers on the bottom of the grip and not inside the crane—that's a batch number—and as for the Chinese... Anyway, that triggered a crisis involving seizure of the rifle, and frantic communications with the three other police forces—who then had to check the auctioneer's catalogue and two dealers' registers.

We have no idea what the cost to the public purse was, and it's for someone else to justify all that palaver being in the national interest, because we can't. If all firearms trading transactions were recorded on one national database, that rifle would have made the transition from auctioneer to dealer to dealer to firearms-certificate holder with one identity—the one the database gave it when it was first entered. We think having a national register is more worthwhile than having policemen racing about ignorant of Farsi numerals. And it would be less costly than teaching the hundreds of policemen, currently involved in trying to close down the gun trade, more about how the gun trade really works (as well as cheaper than Farsi lessons).

Make it all consistent, clear, legal and accountable

The trouble is that the police *like* suspect transactions and poor record-keeping: they create spurious 'reasons' to close dealers down. And the trouble with that is that these really *are* spurious reasons. The law provides only two grounds for removing a dealership from the chief constable's register. One is that the business has already closed; the other is that the trader is a danger to public safety or the peace.

We've encountered that phrase before—'danger to public safety or the peace'. It's the same sole ground as justifies revoking a shotgun certificate. Its meaning is undefined by the Act, but the High Court in *Shepherd* (see page 98) in particular has made it especially clear that the kind of conviction that might result from a suspect transaction or poor record-keeping are not evidence that someone is any danger to public safety or the peace.

Why then do the police continue to close firearms businesses down on spurious, unlawful grounds? How do they keep getting away with it? We don't know, but it's a very British kind of corruption—several stages darker but on the same scale as policemen thinking it's okay to park on double-yellow lines while they have a cup of tea. And we *are* certain that the police will continue ignoring such law as they don't invent, until the government gets to grips with the problem. There are several dozen former firearms dealers waiting for them to do something, each with a claim for lost income resulting from the arbitrary closure of his business.

Wanting to see a modicum of logic and justice in all this, we arrive at the point where it is no longer possible to have the police both issuing and revoking dealerships. It's illegal for them to wear both hats under human-rights law anyway, so it has to be sorted out. What we need is a national system with a national database, managed by people who are properly accountable and who can be sued if they arbitrarily interfere with businesses.

The volume of transactions involving firearms in the UK is way smaller than a minor credit card company would handle on its national database from day to day. The difference is that it would be a bit like banking cash, but having to record the serial numbers of all the notes, so that the next recipient of each of those notes is known to the national database. Perhaps a simpler system would do. But the number of firearms in the UK on certificates, in dealerships and held by exempt persons is way less than a tenth of the number of vehicles that the DVLA manage to keep track of on its database. So, we repeat, we are not asking for any digital miracles here.

What clearly is in the national interest is having a system by which people who need to be registered as dealers can do so efficiently: we believe that need require no more than a fit person certificate, premises certified as secure, and a business plan. Dealers will need the appropriate software to upload transactions and adequate training as to exactly how each transaction should be handled. We would also need to replace Home Office silence with a national handbook that deals unambiguously with each kind of transaction, so that anonymous hand-ins are identifiable, deceased person's effects can be ticked off executors' records, sleepers can be registered for the first time, and so on.

Firearms are firearms. So let's treat them accordingly

The next tangle to unravel is the essentially cosmetic set of distinctions that the current law makes between various kinds, sizes, and mechanics of firearms. This is fundamentally specious. No firearm, within the limits of its ammunition, is potentially more lethal than another. Derrick Bird, in his unfortunate way, showed that lives will not be saved by depriving 60-odd thousand peace-keeping pistol owners of their rightful property.

In 1920, there was one legally-defined category of firearms—and they were called 'firearms'. The 1937 Act introduced a separate category for full-auto (machine) guns. The 1968 Act pigeonholed firearms in three categories: its section 5 for 'prohibited' weapons (such as machine guns), section 2 for shotguns, and section 1 for everything else.. Subsequent legislation has 'elevated' into section 5 some self-loading rifles, some mortars, and some shotguns in 1988; walking stick shotguns in 1993; various types of ammunition in 1993 and 1997; most pistols in 1997; some airguns in 2004; and so it goes on.

A registered firearms dealer is currently authorized to deal in weapons as defined by sections 1 and 2 of the 1968 Act. To deal in section 5 weapons and ammunition, he has to obtain additional authority from the Home Office. To issue the authority, they want to see evidence of 'trading need' in the specific sub-category in section 5. There are only about 50 of these, created by one or other of the numerous bits of legislation since 1968. This is a monumental piece of bureaucracy, but it's all done free of charge by the Home Office. It must keep quite a few people comfortably employed.

A few more jobs for the boys

We take the view that it's all nonsense. Everything over and above ensuring that a dealer has no record of violence or egregious dishonesty, and has secure premises and some head for business, is simply creating jobs for junior bureaucrats and empires for senior ones. We don't know—we hate to think—how many civil servants slave over section 5 applications in the Home Office, checking the minutiae of which already-registered dealer intends doing business with which other dealer and why, before issuing a free authority for a limited number of units, only to have to repeat the whole thing the next week for more units or another sub-category, leaving 48 more subcategories to go over in the coming weeks and months. All of which is a constant restraint on trade, and *none* of which makes our country any safer.

Registration as a firearms dealer should let the dealer trade in all firearms within the meaning of the Act. None of the section 5 restrictions adds anything to public safety: ask one of Derrick Bird's victims. Many sub-categories overlap, making for more contented paper-shuffling and much felling of trees. A Beretta 93R pistol, for in—stance, is both a burst-fire weapon (1988 Act), and a small firearm

(1997 Act). Most submachine guns are both fully automatic and 'small firearms' as defined by barrel length. So—do the Home Office issue you a slot in each of the categories the weapon fits? And do they know how many slots to issue for, say, an M16A1 rifle/40mm under-launcher combination? What difference does it make except to Civil Service employment figures?

It's bureaucracy for its own sake; jobs for the boys. There are probably enough people in the current Home Office department to manage a national database and to issue certificates but, as we know from the late dealer whom they destroyed after the Raoul Moat episode, they aren't accountable. Somebody else should do the work, under strict, publicly-available guidelines.

CHAPTER THIRTEEN

CAN YOU STOP SPREE KILLERS BEFORE THEY START?

S INCE THE LATE 1970s, psychologists and criminologists have had some success in analysing and interpreting the *modus operandi* of serial killers and, in unsolved cases, using the results to create an individual psychological profile that, they hope, will narrow down the investigation to a particular class of people. Profilers with the FBI's Criminal Investigative Analysis Program create a portrait of a perpetrator by using available evidence to try to answer four sets of questions:

- What fantasy or plan, or both, did the murderer have in mind before the act? What can we learn from patterns in his behaviour?
- What type of victim or victims did the murderer select? What was the method and manner of murder? How are these significant?
- Did the murder and body disposal take place all at one scene, or multiple scenes?
- Is the murderer trying to inject himself into the investigation by reacting to media reports or contacting investigators?

The technique hasn't been without controversy, but it has helped to focus and streamline a number of successful serial-murder enquiries. Human beings have a remarkable capacity for variation among individuals, however. So while in hindsight serial killers may tick most boxes in a general psycho-social template, the power of the template is severely curtailed when it comes to *predicting* which individuals, who match the profile, will take up a career in sequential slaying.

Not surprisingly, profilers have tried to create a similar general portrait of spree killers—people like Michael Ryan, Thomas Hamilton and Derrick Bird in the UK, and many more in the US (where the phenomenon is known as 'going postal' after a string of US Post

Office workers went on killing rampages at their places of work). So far, they have failed entirely to find a useful set of dots that, joined up, show that these people have characteristics in common. Spree killers all appear to be one-offs, even in hindsight, and no more predictable than finding the words 'rear admiral' and 'dowser' on the same *curriculum vitae*. In his book *Going Postal* (Snowflake 2007), Mark Ames made a powerful argument for looking less at the spree killer's personal profile and much more closely at the context in which he or she feels driven to strike out. Two crucial points emerge from Ames's analysis. First, and contrary to popular perception, spree killers rarely target their victims randomly, at least in the initial stages of their rampage. Second, they have generally been victimized or bullied—and their chief tormentors are among the first people they kill.

We doubt that such thoughts crossed the minds of civil servants and politicians in the UK after Michael Ryan or Thomas Hamilton ran amok in 1987 and 1996—and Ryan only partly fits the spree-killer's profile. But it is clear now that banning sundry varieties of firearm from private ownership was not the appropriate way to prevent mass murders by shooting. Nothing much, it seems, by way of legislation can prevent this kind of disaster happening occasionally, with or without guns: some people just flip. In reality, the bans of 1988 and 1996 were extensions of an existing policy—not of politicians but of civil servants. Ryan and Hamilton simply provided a 'suitable legislative opportunity' to give that surreptitious agenda the force of law. Uproar in the media and, in 1996/7, the exploitation of public emotion by various parties with questionable motives, gave politicians the fig-leaves they needed to cover their consciences, such as they were.

Where did the system go wrong?

After the Hungerford murders in 1987, vengeful, knee-jerk legislation, based on a secret, unbalanced report drafted by unaccountable bureaucrats and discredited in the 1970s, was likewise hardly a sound approach to the needs of the country. Those of us who had to give up rifles or shoot abroad as a result of that legislation are as surely victims of Michael Ryan as anybody else. The key differences between us and the bereaved are that, on the one hand, we weren't compensated; on the other hand, the balance can still be redressed for those of us still living.

Most people now recognize the bans of 1988 and 1997 as knee-jerk reactions, as revenge on the innocent. The Prime Minister is on record as saying the handgun ban was a mistake. Now that he's in a position to do something about it, we're waiting bright-eyed and bushy-tailed to see if he or the civil servants prove to be in charge of the UK. A lot of innocent people have lost both pastimes and businesses in the years since, and it's time the balance shifted back to the centre. With a following wind, that could be in time for a proper open competition, on British soil, to decide who would best represent our nations in pistol shooting at the 2012 London Olympics.

Before thinking about whether the legislation of 1988 and 1997 was lawful in the light of our constitutional heritage, we should consider whether the system was at fault when Ryan and Hamilton got their certificates; and whether the system we propose in this book, had it been in operation, could have made a difference.

What happened at Hungerford—and before

There was no public enquiry into the Hungerford killings, so much of what we think we know about the build-up to the events of 19 August 1987 may be wrong. What is common ground is that Michael Ryan complied with the firearm certification process as it was at the time, and acquired four guns. One, a .22 Bernadelli Model 69, he traded in before the murders. The other three featured on the day—two shoulder arms (a .30 M1 carbine and a 7.62x39mm Chinese Norinco 56S), and a 9mm Beretta Model 92F pistol. The Norinco was a civilian version of the AK47 Kalashnikov rifle. It came with yellow woodwork, two magazines and in some cases with a bayonet.* The .30 M1 carbine was an American product of the Second World War. Later models came with 30-round magazines, which would fit the earlier versions. The Beretta 92F pistol was adopted by the US army in 1985 to replace the Colt .45 M1911A1.

Ryan's spree started in Wiltshire with the kidnap and murder of a woman who was out picnicking with her two young children in Savernake Forest. On his way back to Hungerford he took a shot at a petrol station window, and once back home he killed his mother and his dog, set light to the house, and shot his car up. He then set off on foot, randomly shooting at anyone he encountered. Among those to die was a police officer sent to find out what was going on. After two hours, 30 people had been shot, 16 fatally. Having fired 119 rounds, Ryan was almost out of ammunition by then and hiding in his old school, surrounded by police. He then shot himself.

---

* While that sounds odd, it's a curious fact of shooting that fitting a bayonet to a rifle enlarges the 'group'—the area within which a consistently aimed shot lands—and some competitions require that bayonets are fitted. This helps to widen the range of scores and so distinguishes the best shooter from the nearly best.

There is no logic to be found in his actions, although it may be belatedly useful to know that he had few friends and a reputation for sulkiness as a child, and was often bullied. He responded by shooting at neighbours' children with an airgun. His indulgent mother spoiled him rotten throughout his life and probably, thereby, oppressed him emotionally. He remained a solitary; he seems never to have had a girlfriend (although he told yarns about a *fiancée*—he had a rich fantasy life, which included having been in 2 Para and having a pilot's licence). He did not succeed in any of the trades or vocations he tried to take up, and was unemployed for long stretches. According to former workmates he had a habit of carrying a loaded pistol everywhere, tucked into his waistband.

The failure to hold a public enquiry, uniquely among the multiple (and sometimes single) fatal disasters of that period, has always made it look as if the powers-that-be knew something they didn't want scrutinized. We have no opinion on the truth of that supposition.

Did the certification system fail? Changes made later to the criteria for joining Home Office-approved clubs—the extended probation period in particular—would, we think, have discouraged this character. He probably wouldn't have completed the probation, and under yet later rules wouldn't, therefore, have been given a ticket. But as things stood at the time, neither he nor the police seem to have done anything out of order—his criminal record consisted of one speeding ticket, he had a hefty Chubb safe for his guns, a reputation for being unusually safety-conscious on the range. If there was a failure, it lay outside the system: for some reason, no one alerted the police to his carry-piece, his shooting up roadsigns, or his home-made bombs, whose effectiveness he demonstrated at least once.

Some evidence emerged after the events to suggest that Ryan also had a couple of off-ticket firearms; neither of the guns he was reportedly seen with was ever found, and they may have been de-acts or replicas. But a third off-ticket firearm was discovered in the burnt-out remains of his house. So it would appear that, had Ryan not chosen to go the legal route he did, he still had a means of arming himself for any shooting spree he'd set his heart on.

No angel to watch over him—or his victims

The lesson we would draw from the Hungerford murders is that Michael Ryan was not closely mentored at his clubs. He wasn't the subject of direct training, as such, so he never had someone to whom he could open his mind. Neither was there a someone taking a close interest in his attitude to guns or the shooting sports. Every instruc-

tor, in every kind of coaching, will sooner or later come across someone unsuited to the activity they're trying out.

Such people don't finish their courses—they give up, for any
number of reasons—it might be the expense, or standing on an open
range in December, or simply not the fun they thought it would be.
People who don't seem safe on the firing point are quietly discouraged from going further. At worst, they're refused full membership
of the club they've joined as probationers.

In the 1990s, with a tighter and longer probation period in place,
more than half of all probationary members did not stick with shooting to the point of applying for a certificate. They came, they tried, it
wasn't for them, or they weren't for other club members. We suspect
Michael Ryan would not have lasted through such a probation period
or the close scrutiny of trainers and examiners.

Under our system, he would have had the basic character certificate, but would not have achieved a certificate of competence for
any class of firearm. That would have left him with either no
weapons, or having to resort to a supplier of weapons from the unregistered pool. Which rather underlines one of our themes in this
book: the more weapons that can be brought into a system of registration, the better. Banning things, be they guns or anything else, is
really a way to abandon any pretence at control of them, and the
people who want to have them.

The scourge of Dunblane: a man with a history

Thomas Hamilton was in a rather different position. He was quite
well known to his community, and he had baggage. His independent
boys' clubs had quite a turnover of members, so plenty of children
who had been to them had also grown up in the area and knew him,
as did their parents. He was also known as a shooter, although not a
particularly active one.

In the run-up to the murders in 1996, his life was difficult. He had
financial problems. Whispers, that his interest in young boys was not
entirely noble, were rife. It's well-known that he was having difficulty
keeping his athletics club going—he was up against a mixture of officials obstructing his access to public space, and parental hostility,
which may have been fuelling the official position. In response, he
complained vehemently at every perceived persecution that officialdom heaped on him: he was 'difficult'. Police on the ground (and a
lot of shooting-club officials) seem to have been aware of what he
was like and what was being said about him.

Could any of that have been articulated into a reason for revoking or (in 1995) refusing to renew his firearms certificate? Not really, we think. Hamilton may have been touchy (perhaps with good reason) but wasn't apparently of intemperate habits or unsound mind, and had done nothing violent to indicate any danger to the public or the peace. There was no hard evidence of any misconduct in running his clubs, so it would have been difficult to justify the conclusion that he was 'otherwise unfitted', at least if he appealed the revocation— which, to judge from his habitual stroppiness with officialdom, he most likely would have.

In 1995, too, Hamilton was, as required since 1991, a member of an approved shooting club. Two years later, however, he was not. A Shooter's Rights Association briefing, written the day after the murders and based on speaking to shooters in the area, says:

> In 1987 Hamilton joined the Stirling Rifle and Pistol Club, moving from his previous club and presumably already in possession of a firearm certificate. He did not renew his membership when it expired about a month ago, and had approached three other clubs in the area, the last being the Callander Rifle and Pistol Club, about the time his membership of the Stirling Club expired. All three attempts were unsuccessful, and it is known that Callander refused him because he was unable to supply a supporting statement from a previous club or person of good standing in the community vouching for his character and integrity. (This is a requirement of the club concerned, as elsewhere, and his inability to supply it resulted, naturally, in his being refused even probationary membership).

So what was Hamilton's problem with shooting clubs as 1995 turned into 1996? We don't know precisely, but we do know that clubs are social entities, not just shooting galleries. Every club will be familiar with square peg syndrome. Some people can be the life and soul of one party, but be quite pernicious at another.

In our clubs, we meet the other members when they have loaded firearms to hand. We don't want to share the premises with anyone we don't trust with a gun. Dealers are in exactly the same position. No gunshop wants a customer who's flaky enough to come in shooting one day because somebody upset him. We weed these characters out. Our test is based on reality, rather than on manipulating the paperwork. That three clubs didn't fancy Hamilton as a member suggests that somehow or other he exuded the wrong atmosphere, even if in a manner no one could quite put their finger on—an impression borne out by members who gave evidence to Lord Cullen. And it's here that the police's intelligence fell down.

A tale of a ticket, and a mysteriously missing file

Lord Cullen says that Hamilton was first issued a firearm certificate on 14 February 1977, to shoot .22 pistol with the Callander club and on other suitable ranges. He bought a Vostok and shortly thereafter traded it for a Smith and Wesson revolver. At the time, he could have taken a day membership at Callander—or any commercial range—without belonging to the club itself. His certificate was renewed, says Lord Cullen, on time every three years.

As Hamilton hadn't become a member of another club after his Stirling membership expired, the police could have cancelled his certificate until he got in somewhere else: that would have meant putting his guns into store with a dealer. Also, without a club, he had nowhere to practise. Given that he was not well regarded in the clubs, it seems that by March 1996 he had no officially-acceptable 'good reason' for possessing firearms at all, but the police did not act. It seems they were simply unaware of his lapsed membership at Stirling, and the club was under no obligation to tell them of it.

The renewal of Hamilton's ticket in 1995 has been the subject of some comment. Everyone who asked at the time, after the murders, was told that the police file had gone missing. Interesting: make of it what you will.

That file wasn't put on the desk of Deputy Chief Constable (DCC) McMurdo when he renewed Hamilton's certificate in 1995. The police seem to have had an open goal at this point, and missed it. Officers on the ground who had met Hamilton for his 1992 renewal had already recommended not renewing his certificate (one described him as "a scheming, devious and deceitful individual who is not to be trusted"), but that advice was overridden by a more senior officer, on the not unreasonable grounds that Hamilton had not been convicted of any crime, and a complaint regarding his behaviour toward one of his boys' club members was unlikely to be pursued by the Procurator Fiscal. Reports of the adverse impressions of other officers who had contact with Hamilton weren't lodged either in his firearms file or in his criminal intelligence file. As the firearms file—had it *already* gone missing?—wasn't shown to the DCC (as was standard practice) when he was expected to authorize renewal, he was unable to revise his opinion. In Lord Cullen's judgement the DCC took an unduly narrow view of what might make someone 'unfitted' to have firearms (for instance, a relevant conviction). Consequently he renewed Hamilton's ticket pretty much on the nod, despite having been, in his own words, a "beneficiary of Mr Hamilton's vindictive correspondence" in the past. One may reasonably suggest that he should have looked again at the file before scribbling his signature; and if everything that should have been in it *had* been in it, he might have had second thoughts.

But we would also observe that, despite the failings of the police filing system here, DCC McMurdo's overall view was reasonable and civilised, whatever Lord Cullen implied. A decision to revoke, or not to renew, Hamilton's firearms certificate was not justified by any solid evidence that he had misused firearms, or that he was actually or potentially violent. Hamilton does appear to have been something of a pervert, albeit a relatively controlled one. But to refuse someone a firearms certificate on the grounds of their sexual tastes, however illegal and repugnant, smacks of thought policing. We know of one chap, of some renown as a thespian, who was twice caught doing rather revolting things with other chaps in public lavatories: that didn't stop him getting a firearm certificate and, actually, becoming a fair marksman and stalwart helper-out at his club. So we're disinclined to lay the 'blame for Dunblane' entirely at the police's feet.

If the police *had* become aware of Hamilton's lapsed club membership in 1996 and revoked his certificate, and Hamilton had asked us about appealing the decision to the courts, we'd have told him that club membership demonstrated 'good reason' for target shooting: so he should find a club that would have him, and then apply for the certificate back. Given the downhill track his life was on at the time, we suspect he wouldn't have had the time to devote to getting into a club. So, once his guns had gone into secure storage, he would have put the issue on the back burner.

The way it could have worked

Of course the inaccessibility of his pistols may not have prevented him slaughtering a lot of innocent children: as we showed in our Introduction, spree killers don't depend on firearms for their grisly work. That spree killers aren't predictable, besides, is a truism that should also lighten the burden on the police's decision to let Hamilton continue to have a firearm certificate. If there was a fault in the system, it was one of attitude and intelligence. If the police had had the wit to seek opinions of Hamilton from his fellow shooters and from the dealers who sold him guns and ammunition, they might have had a better picture of him. They might also have been alerted to his desperate, repeatedly unsuccessful attempts to be accepted by into a new shooting club, and drawn the appropriate conclusions.

Let's now look at Hamilton through the rose-tinted glasses of our proposals for reforming the legislation. He had a firearm certificate, so his basic character reference and security would have been in place, as had, let's assume, his certificate of competence for handguns. But, he was coming up to renewal in February 1995. Would anyone in his local clubs have given him a certificate of competence then? We think not.

People in the Callander Club did not want to support his application for membership. These people knew what he was like much better, we think, than the police did. At each certificate renewal, we would want to see a renewed certificate of competence, from a qualified club or shoot official, for each class of firearms held; naturally some people in the countryside fall outside that condition, but they still have peers to vouch for them, and farmers have a union. Who would have signed it for Hamilton? Not people in his club, we think. His local dealer? We think dealers are an excellent source of wisdom about what turns their customers' propellers. It's the Home Office who don't trust them. By taking that position they deny law enforcement a useful source of intelligence.

We think that under our proposed way of doing things, Hamilton would have not have had his certificate renewed—or, had it been renewed because the file was missing, it would have been revoked some time later as concerns about him mounted. (We've pointed out before that his sudden accumulation of ammunition would have shown up and invited attention if it had appeared on a centralized database.) Suitably discouraged, he would have focussed on the rest of his life falling apart. He *might* have got things together and restored his reputation in the local community—in which case his murders, which remind us of the Pied Piper's revenge on Hamlyn, wouldn't have happened. If they had, it would have been through some other lethal means. Remember, the original Pied Piper didn't have a gun.

The non-mysterious invisibility of Derrick Bird

We should tread lightly around Derrick Bird, simply because at the time of writing there are official enquiries under way that we would not want to usurp. What we knew about him on the day from people in Whitehaven was that he was not known locally as a shooter. He was unknown to the club there, and the local dealer said he didn't know him. We surmised (correctly as it turned out) that if he wasn't a target shooter, he probably had his guns for pest control on private property somewhere. As we have mentioned before, it's possible to get into that kind of shooting without having a mentor. As a result, few people knew what he was like with guns, and what he knew or thought he knew about his guns may have been self-taught.

The ACPO report by ACC Adrian Whiting says that Bird first got a shotgun certificate in 1974; there is no indication that he let it lapse at any point, so that's one grant and nine renewals in 25-odd years. He got his firearm certificate in 2007. The police, therefore, had the opportunity to talk to him 11 times: but there weren't any contra-indications and, in the kind of shooting that was his 'good reason', there were no mentors or club secretaries with whom to discuss things. Within the terms of our proposal, there would probably have been nothing to raise any suspicions either. Was there anything else that anyone else could have done, either under the current régime or a reformed one?

Most people tend not to know who among us have firearms. Few shooters advertise themselves, so if nobody who worked with Bird knew he had guns, that would not be surprising. That he wasn't known to the local dealer suggests either that he acquired ammunition only rarely, or was not a memorable person. Where and when he acquired ammunition for his rifle will be a matter of record on his certificate; shotgun cartridges are not exclusively sold by the gun trade and in rural areas are available in a variety of retail outlets.

Like Michael Ryan and Thomas Hamilton, Derrick Bird seemed to come out of nowhere. We don't know much about Michael Ryan, but we do know Thomas Hamilton was being painted into a corner because his one-man athletics schemes for children in the community weren't getting approval from officialdom, not to mention parents. One rumour says that had he not gone shooting at Dunblane Primary School on 13 March 1996, he would have been home to meet bailiffs coming to evict him. Derrick Bird, we understand, was being bullied.

There seems to be no way to foresee and prevent people like these from running amok. Under our proposal for dealing with certificate grants and renewals, Derrick Bird would see someone for a certificate of competence every five years. That means an experienced person would see him using his guns and listen to him. That, we think, is better than just asking for someone, who may have nothing to do with the shooting sports, to counter-sign an application form.

If you can't prevent a problem, you may be able to cure it

We have to wonder at the number of times spree shootings are reported. Globally, it's not often, but what's interesting is the places they occur. In Killeen, Texas, for example, on 16 October 1991, George Jo Hennard drove his pick-up truck through the front window of Luby's Cafeteria, where some 80 patrons were minding their own business. Hennard yelled "This is what Bell County has done to me!" and then, wielding two semi-auto pistols, proceeded to shoot 23 people dead and wound 20 more before killing himself. The massacre directly inspired the Texas legislature to make it much easier to carry a concealed, loaded handgun in public (once one's passed a not-too-onerous test of competence). The new law took effect on 1 January 1996, and by 2010 nearly half a million people had taken advantage of it. If you go into a restaurant with 80 patrons in Texas now, the chances are that your fellow-diners include at least two Concealed-Handgun License holders, *and they will be armed.* In contrast, American schools are, by federal law, gun-free zones, so every spree killer who opens fire at a school or college in the US can be reasonably certain that there won't be any return fire.

England is full of unarmed people. So is Scotland. None of our home-grown spree-killers had any prospect of meeting return fire, so they went about their plan for the day certain that they were not going to be interrupted. There is anecdotal evidence from Hungerford that a firearm certificate holder could have shot at Michael Ryan, but didn't, being uncertain of his legal position. The police on the ground at the time got to revolvers quickly enough, but were not able to close with Ryan, who in any case had lost the will to live before the police boxed him in. It has always seemed odd that Thomas Hamilton's spree ended so quickly. He hadn't run out of ammunition or targets, so was he working to some timing of his own? We don't know; possibly he interpreted the first adult intervention as an armed response and reacted as he'd planned. He may have known how long an armed response was likely to take and set himself a time limit.

Derrick Bird seems to have run out of steam. Having damaged his vehicle and bailed out of it, he had limited options on foot. We don't yet know whether he was out of ammunition, but we feel sure that he knew he was outclassed by his pursuers and did not want a confrontation with them.

Our view is that such incidents, already rare and generally unlikely, could be even less likely if a greater possibility existed of an armed intervention. If someone had got a shot off at Derrick Bird, it might well have interrupted his train of thought, even if it hadn't hit him. A damaged windscreen or tyre might have made him feel vulnerable. Then he might well have disengaged and fled. Maybe.

When two laws conflict, spree killers thrive

The point we have to confront here is the conflict between the history of our rights and our current legislation. There may be no conflict at all, according to one line of thought. Firearm certificates and trading registrations were introduced in 1920 to regulate sporting guns, not those kept for defence. Huge numbers of firearms were not registered in 1920 because they didn't need to be. They were not kept for target shooting or hunting; they were kept for protection, as they had been since the 1689 clarification of that right. In 1909, when police were in hot pursuit of robbers in Tottenham, they cheerfully borrowed pistols and revolvers from public-spirited, routinely-armed passers-by.

With the passage of time, however, this seems to have been forgotten; unregistered firearms were rechristened the 'illegal pool', and anyone found possessing a 'prohibited' small firearm—a handgun, in common parlance—these days gets a five-year gaol term without passing Go. So what became of the right to arms as enshrined in the Bill of Rights?

According to anecdotal evidence, it hasn't entirely been forgotten. We hear that many street gangsters caught carrying unregistered guns are not charged. This is because they have, same as the rest of us, a common law right to protect themselves, and—crucially—have had the wit to point this out to arresting officers. There is a difference between 'unregistered' and 'illegal', after all. There is also some evidence to suggest that when a person uses a firearm in self-defence, their common law rights are still recognized. A problem arises merely because various questionable laws put obstructions in the way of your possessing a firearm and appropriate ammunition against the day you may need to use them. English law is full of paradoxes like this. It's legal to clear a way through an obstructed or overgrown public footpath, for example, but it's *not* legal to go for a walk kitted out with the tools—wirecutters, secaturs—you may need for the job. Presumably ramblers are supposed to use their teeth to cut barbed wire. Back at the question of defensive firearms, we observe that the Bill of Rights hasn't been repealed. The various Firearms Acts, therefore, do not override or implicitly repeal it.

The old laws are always the best

The validity of the Bill of Rights came up in the context of the case of the 'Metric Martyrs' (costermongers wicked enough to persist in selling bananas by the pound, instead of the kilo). The judgement, dated 18 February 2002 and delivered by Lord Justice Laws, includes these comments in paragraphs 62 and 63:

> In the present state of its maturity the common law has come to recognize that there exist rights which should properly be classified as constitutional or fundamental: see for example such cases as Simms

[2000] 2 AC 115 per Lord Hoffmann at 131, Pierson v Secretary of State [1998] AC 539, Leech [1994] QB 198, Derbyshire County Council v Times Newspapers Ltd. [1993] AC 534, and Witham [1998] QB 575. And from this a further insight follows. We should recognize a hierarchy of Acts of Parliament: as it were "ordinary" statutes and "constitutional" statutes. The two categories must be distinguished on a principled basis. In my opinion a constitutional statute is one which (a) conditions the legal relationship between citizen and State in some general, overarching manner, or (b) enlarges or diminishes the scope of what we would now regard as fundamental constitutional rights. (a) and (b) are of necessity closely related: it is difficult to think of an instance of (a) that is not also an instance of (b). **The special status of constitutional statutes follows the special status of constitutional rights. Examples are the Magna Carta, the Bill of Rights 1689, the Act of Union, the Reform Acts which distributed and enlarged the franchize, the HRA, the Scotland Act 1998 and the Government of Wales Act 1998. The ECA clearly belongs in this family.** It incorporated the whole corpus of substantive Community rights and obligations, and gave overriding domestic effect to the judicial and administrative machinery of Community law. It may be there has never been a statute having such profound effects on so many dimensions of our daily lives. The ECA is, by force of the common law, a constitutional statute.

63 Ordinary statutes may be impliedly repealed. Constitutional statutes may not. For the repeal of a constitutional Act or the abrogation of a fundamental right to be effected by statute, the court would apply this test: is it shown that the legislature's actual—not imputed, constructive or presumed—intention was to effect the repeal or abrogation? I think the test could only be met by express words in the later statute, or by words so specific that the inference of an actual determination to effect the result contended for was irresistible. The ordinary rule of implied repeal does not satisfy this test. Accordingly, it has no application to constitutional statutes. I should add that in my judgment general words could not be supplemented, so as to effect a repeal or significant amendment to a constitutional statute, by reference to what was said in Parliament by the minister promoting the Bill pursuant to Pepper v Hart [1993] AC 593. A constitutional statute can only be repealed, or amended in a way which significantly affects its provisions touching fundamental rights or otherwise the relation between citizen and State, by unambiguous words on the face of the later statute.

To put it bluntly, the Firearms Acts, from 1920 onward, have not amended the Bill of Rights with respect to your right to defend life, liberty and property, with a firearm if necessary. These rights are upheld as inviolate by the European Convention on Human Rights, to which our government is a signatory; much of it is re-articulated into statute law by the Human Rights Act 1998.

We've arrived at the uncomfortable position in the UK where we have a complicated series of Firearms Acts, which don't affect your right to have a firearm, and have been thoroughly discredited by the way they've been perniciously administered. That we should be thinking in such terms is a consequence of the way the legislation has been progressively tightened, to no useful effect. If you over-tighten the wheelnuts on a vehicle, chances are you'll strip the threads and lose the wheel. That's what's happening with firearms legislation—it's too tight and the wheel's coming off.

CHAPTER FOURTEEN
A SYSTEM THAT WORKS

THERE'S ALWAYS a way of fixing things. In principle, we have no objection to a system of certificates and dealer registrations to keep track of who owns which firearms. But it has to be a system that does something worth while, and does it economically, and without conflicting with the common law and human rights. It also has to be proof against being *taken* to override, repeal or replace common law and human rights legislation.

The current system purports to 'control' what we can own, where and when we can use each item, and imposes draconian penalties for the slightest deviation from the constraints—many of which are administrative and victimless rather than legislative. Whom does that serve? Not the users, for sure. It keeps a lot of bureaucrats and chairbound policemen in well-paid work, and generates firearms statistics to worry politicians and justify the salaries of the bureaucrats and police. It also helps to bump up firearms 'crime' statistics, which in turn help to justify the existence of police arsenals of unregistered weapons—which they keep and bear under a common-law exemption that, they seem to have forgotten, also applies to the public.

Does it do anything else? Good question. Certainly having a system of certificates acts as a barrier to instant access: you can't buy a gold-plated Kalashnikov on impulse in Harrods because you like its colour. A recent change in the law restricts the sale of air-soft toys to those who can show that they have appropriate public-liability insurance when playing with such things. That is actually the sort of system we have in mind. Under it, you would need to go through a process of training and preparation to show that you are a paid-up good guy, and Big Brother knows who you are. After that, the door should be as wide open to you as it is closed to those who have not been initiated.

We have woven our principles—what we think is worth while—

into this book, putting each proposal in context. To summarize that, our view is that the common-law exemption from registration and certification is all very well, but it's complicated to prove at the point of sale. It's no hardship to have a system that registers firearms owners. However, registration must not conflict with our common law rights or with the protection we enjoy under European law. Essentially this means that registration can't be used to confiscate firearms held for defence.

Certificates should be issued by a national body, suitably account-able to the courts and/or a purpose-built tribunal. We think that should be an agency, operating to clear, published guidance firmly based on the legislation and case law. The initial application from interested parties of any age is simply for a fit person certificate. When issued, that will show that the holder is not a prohibited person under the Act, and he or she can thus join any shooting club that will accept the holder, or sign up for any shooting course.

To own firearms, shooters will obtain a certificate of competence for each class of firearm that they wish to own and will install or rent security that must be certified as adequate. Referring the security validation and certificate of competence for a class of firearm to the issuing authority enables the basic certificate to be extended so that firearms in the class or classes for which the individual is certified competent can be acquired. The total number of firearms acquired in the classes the individual is authorized to possess should not exceed the number that the security can hold.

What's a 'class' of firearm? Simplicity is of the essence

That's easy enough. Shotguns are a class of firearms. There is no point or need to distinguish action types, barrel lengths, or any of the other bureaucratic differentials that have crept in over time. Shotguns all do the same thing. Those that do it with cartridges all do the same thing regardless of action type; some are muzzle-loaded and use dif-ferent ammunition. It may be worth splitting certificates of compe-tence within the class—but of that, more below.

Other classes are: smallbore rifles; fullbore rifles; smallbore pis-tols; fullbore pistols; loose ammunition pistols; muzzle-loaded rifles and shotguns; and automatic weapons.

Firearms, we have to repeat, are inanimate objects, designed to launch a projectile. The families we divide them into above are based on the kind of ranges that would be provided for each. All shotguns do the same thing, for example. It does not matter what the barrel length is, or the magazine capacity, or any of the other differences that are apparent when it's photographed. The range considerations remain the same. The shot will go only so far, and the size of a range's safety area is unaffected regardless of whether it's a pump-action gun with a 20-inch barrel or a best English side-by-side with 32-inch barrels. The wooden stock on an English gun does not alter the range of the cartridge. Neither does the folding metal stock on an Italian repeater.

The choice of barrel length and action type is precisely that: a choice. We know some politicians worry about black plastic stocks and other cosmetic effects, but giving them tablets to calm them down is more cost-effective than maintaining illogical legislation.

In a free market, the choice of action type and barrel length is decided by what works best for the owners' intentions and his pocket. Prior to 1988, the Country Landowners' Association's annual game fair featured a 75-bird duck flush sponsored by Famous Grouse whisky, competed in by three-man teams. Because this tended to be won by Remington 1100 owners, they were given a separate class of their own, which is nature's way of telling us how good that particular repeating gun is for that kind of shooting.

Other kinds of shooting favour other configurations; same as some outdoor clothing is suited to one season more than another. And the folding shoulder stocks Douglas Hogg hated so much? Repeating guns tend to be much longer than doubles and don't break down for transporting. The folding stock lets you get the thing in a car boot; with a rigid stock, some such guns have to ride as front-seat passengers or on the roof rack (not ideal). Some American folding shotgun stocks are stamped 'law enforcement only': maybe that's where they got the idea from—to limit them to our servants only, and make them feel more important. More likely, they were inspired by gangster movies, which featured villains with fancy shotguns more often than did actual crimes.

Does crossing a border strangely change one's character?

We do not see any point in trying to maintain the artificial prohibitions of the past. They put us at odds with most other countries, for a start. We can shoot pistols in Northern Ireland, semi-automatic rifles in Jersey and machine guns in Belgium, so why not here? We still have many of the facilities, the various bans and prohibitions contribute nothing to public safety, and all are at odds with our common law. And what exactly changes in our nature when we fly to Arizona, spend three weeks legally carrying a loaded pistol, shoot it, and an Uzi and an AK-47 on a public range a couple of times, and then fly back to the UK? Does the bump of aircraft tyres on Gatwick's dreary rainswept runway suddenly make us sprout horns and grow tails and turn our feet to hooves? When the Firearms Act 1988 was implemented in 1989, the effect was that the gun trade was the first industry into recession, 18 months ahead of everyone else. This time, and by sorting out who can buy what, the gun trade could lead the country back to prosperity.

First train; train some more; and then keep practising

Firearms, as we said, can broadly be classified in terms of the kind of range they'll be used on or at. But there are subcategories too, for which it's worth establishing distinct training courses and certificates of competence. Take shotguns: competence with any one cartridge gun stands you in fairly good stead for understanding any other. Most safety issues revolve around what the ammunition does, after all, although we'd want certificates of competence to show that a shooter knows how to handle every kind of cartridge gun from a sidelock to a semi-auto. But some shotguns are muzzle-loaders. There are no cartridges: you load the powder, pack it with wadding, add loose shot and an overshot wad and them prime the pan or cap the nipple. Regardless of what you know about shooting a cartridge gun safely, you'd rather take a separate course before taking a flintlock out by yourself, wouldn't you?

The shooting disciplines form a broad church, in which many organizations became governing bodies before the Competitions Act, providing specialist knowledge and training to their members. We regard it as crucial that everyone is trained to use the firearms they are subsequently authorized to possess. Hardly anyone drives competently and safely without proper prior training. And that's just on the road: people skilled in driving 4x4s on mud, snow, or sand have either learned at their farmer Dad's knee, or have taken a course. The same principles hold true for firearms. As there's some overlap in the weapons and disciplines that shooting organizations cover, they should all be providing training modules and be equally recognized for their efforts. We suspect that Michael Ryan, Thomas Hamilton and Derrick Bird had little training, by which we mean limited contact with a coach who might have been able to pick up any evidence of poor attitude, lax discipline, or deteriorating stability.

We say this knowing that compulsory training, when introduced to the Scout movement in the 1960s, caused a great deal of anger among very experienced leaders who really thought that they couldn't be taught anything. It's not a common attitude though; most competent firearms instructors and experienced shooters like nothing more than getting on someone else's course as a student. What makes it difficult for UK shooters now is the cost, which is often compounded by having to get to sparse facilities several counties from home. That will change as training becomes the gold standard. Scouting suffered in this respect because so many courses were at Gilwell, near Chingford, which used to be in Essex. Shooting has the same problem with Bisley, in Surrey. In any event, it's easier to get an instructor to the local range than it is ship 30 students to Bisley, but trade and commerce would sort things out to the advantage of all.

Taking shotguns first, their uses really split into only two classes—targets and hunting. Within those two classes are numerous disciplines for which there are already courses. Our view is that a certificate of competence in one discipline opens the door to all, but—as we remarked earlier—the training, and the consequent certificate of competence, should cover *all* types of shotgun, so that people are familiar with their different mechanics and handling characteristics. The separate certificate of competence we suggest for muzzle-loaders would be necessary anyway, to get the separate gunpowder licence issued under the Explosives Act, unless—dammit, why not streamline everything?—the certificate of competence for muzzle-loaders included an exemption from the need to hold the separate explosives licence. Beyond that, you won't get the maximum benefit from specialoist activities such as wildfowling without proper instruction. King George VI took lessons from the locals in Norfolk, blazing a trail humbler folk can follow.

Shotgun shooting, it is said, is an art; pistol shooting is a skill, and rifle shooting is a science. Machine gunning is noisy and expensive. The differences between them are like those between motorcycles, cars and lorries. Different techniques have to be learned to get the best out of them, although all the basic rules remain the same. Anybody who takes a clay pigeon course is going to be out of his depth at a practical shotgun event and vice versa, albeit only in the finer points of technique and the etiquette of the activity. But the skills learned about the ammunition and how to discharge it safely are transferable, as it's all shotgun pellets.

Horses for courses; guns for ranges

We split other firearms into the families that ranges have been constructed for. It's about the safe use of the ammunition in families of similarity; shotguns all fire pellets that have a short range and most shotgunning uses the sky as a backstop. Well, not a backstop, but shotgun cartridges are designed to be fired into the sky at moving targets. The pellets run out of momentum and fall to the ground within 300 yards in the case of sizes 6 and down.

With rifles and pistols, the bullets will go much further—several miles in some cases—so every kind of bulleted ammunition is used in conjunction with some means of stopping the projectile after it has done what it was supposed to. That may mean a metal backstop, or sand, loose or bagged. Old tyres filled with sand or a good earth bank. Some ranges have danger areas which may be on land or may be the open sea. Shooters in the field have to make their own assessment of the safety of their backstop for every shot.

On all courses, whatever the weapon, the shooter should be seen to be safe and mannerly on the range (this is basic to gaining any certificate of competence), and should have some basic instruction in techniques for accurate shooting; bad habits learned early are like red-wine stains: difficult to eradicate, and frustrating for perfectionists.

Training with a smallbore rifle in any one of the disciplines for which they are used is good grounding for any of the other disciplines. In the case of the venerable .22 rifle, for example, there are four basic shooting positions (stand, sit, kneel, prone—usually taught in reverse order to that), and general rules for aiming, trigger control, sight picture, and so on are common to all. Just about everything else is about etiquette or mechanics—basic safety and range manners, how to adjust sights, use the magazine or the sling, semi-auto action *versus* bolt-action: so one course mostly fits all target shooters.

We recommend a separate course before using .22 rifles for pest control. Much of the difference is classroom work and to do with what can be shot, how and when, but a course that covered the additional burden of guaranteeing that every shot in the field is a safe one in the countryside would be well worth while.

As with rifles, so with pistols

Smallbore pistols are used in various disciplines, with variations on the size and shape of the target and how far away it is, same as with rifles. No .22 pistol discipline involves any position other than standing, so one course is the starting point for all the variations that are to be found. As with .22 rifles, shooters should be competent in using semi-autos, revolvers, and single-shot pistols.

Shooting fullbore pistol, apart from accommodating the louder bang and heftier recoil, involves various stances, all of which should be covered on basic courses. It's also different from shooting .22 pistol to the extent that fullbore encompasses one- and two-handed and holster work, and faster reaction times in some competitions. One thorough course, once again, is a good entry point for all the subsequent variations. Competence should be shown with both revolvers and semi-auto pistols.

To maintain public safety—the health of 'innocent bystanders'—a separate course and certificate is worth having for those who are going to carry pistols discreetly in public. Choosing both the firearm and the carry rig can be complicated, but it's even more important for armed citizens to understand when a firearm can *and can not* legally be used to protect life, liberty, chastity and property *defensively*. It's a somewhat different set of rules from those that apply to policing: constitutionally, the citizen's rights and powers are more limited than those of the paid public servant. Tony Martin did not know where the boundaries of his rights to defend his property lay, and landed in gaol. Had he had the right training beforehand, he would have known how to conduct himself and his defensive operation lawfully.

Such people as might carry in public would not need to belong to a club, although there are advantages in their doing so, so that they can practise. The organizations that have provided this kind of training in the past do not need to be clubs either, although some have been as a flag of convenience to gain access to facilities. Better if they flew under their own colours in future.

We regard loose ammunition pistols as worth a separate certificate, partly because of the need for a black powder licence issued under the Explosives Act (or an exemption from it via the specific certificate of competence), but mostly because it is the pipe-smoking end of the shooting sports. Anyone trained on modern fullbore handguns will find little transferable technical knowledge when it comes to getting a cap and ball revolver shooting. It's like knowing your car thoroughly and then being given a 1928 steamroller to fire up.

Competence in using a fullbore rifle splits comfortably into target and field; courses for the latter tend to be specific to a quarry species, such as deer, but one course based on deer would stand the graduate in good stead if his next outing is after boar or foxes.

Our view then is that a certificate of competence, linked to a fit person certificate and a security approval is all that is needed for the individual to buy such firearms as he has been trained to use and as many as fit in his security. That provides a solid framework for future certificate holders and does away will all the pointless job creation that we've been paying for through fees and taxes.

The full firearm certificate should also authorize the holder to permit any of his firearms to be used under his instruction and in his presence by any fit-person certificate holder. That does away with the need to issue certificates authorizing possession of firearms to people under 18, to the relief of all those perpetual worriers.

We've said it before—firearms are firearms: treat them as such

The system of certificates of competence that we propose does away with the artificial distinction between section 2 shotguns and section 1 firearms. It also does away with the distinction of section 5 'prohibited' weapons, which we view as redundant under this system, and as a fatuous, spiteful invasion of liberty under the present one.

All this opens the question as to whether or not we would need Home Office approval for shooting clubs at all. It's now so limited anyway that it has little validity, constraining as it does the network of facilities at which only a minority of the firearms still 'legal' get used. It would make more sense for a national body to register clubs for the purpose (or purposes) for which they exist. You can either know who is doing what through a system or registration or have nothing and remain blissfully ignorant of what the public do. The latter works perfectly well in other countries, but may not suit the English way ("hanging on in quiet desperation", as someone said).

Before leaving this aspect of the topic, it's worth remembering that *shooting* firearms is not the only good reason for being their registered keeper. There are museum and reference collections, private collections, trophies of war and other souvenir categories to be accommodated by some means; such possession does not usually authorize ammunition, and a basic course in law and safe handling would probably suffice. People who handle firearms need to know how to check them for ammunition—it's not unusual to find antique muzzle-loaders with a charge still in them more than a century after they were last used.

What we advocate is streamlining. Most certificates currently on issue are to people with whom neither society nor the government have a problem. If you want to spot the dodgy certificate holders, the first thing to do is to simplify the process for the rest. Then, and only then, will oddballs stand out further. They don't at the moment because the police regard all certificate holders as target criminals, as investigative opportunities, and as potential meat for the wheels of justice, from which they can generate self-justifying statistics.

With such an approach, nobody can spot any real danger. But if the system's generally sleek then lumps and mange will show up, and questions can be generated. We mentioned the Farsi farce of the Persian rifle earlier. It would not become an issue under our system, so the police would have time to look at more interesting anomalies, like Thomas Hamilton emerging from several years' hibernation as a suddenly enthusiastic ammunition buyer in 1995. Come to that, a computer system should have spotted him going dormant in the first place, thus generating an enquiry; his sudden purchase of large quantities of ammunition would have provoked more interest. And then one could wonder about which club he was using the stuff at.

Who's going to manage all this?

What sort of body would or could issue firearms certificates on a national basis? That's an interesting question. The existing bodies—police and Home Office—have lost all credibility, pursuing extra-legal agendas and trying everything possible to avoid doing their purported jobs. They have done untold damage to businesses and individuals, and it will take years to sort out their mess and to compensate people whose lives have been disrupted, often quite cynically, and almost always unaccountably, by the existing régime.

So who or what might be up for the job? The current government isn't fond of quangoes, which in general is fair enough, but frustrating from our point of view. The model—the actual candidate—for a national firearms agency that we have in mind is a quango: the Security Industry Authority (SIA).

The SIA handles the 'fit person' qualification when someone applies for the various badges they issue. As it happens, they use the same criterion of 'danger to public safety or the peace' as the Firearms Act in this, and when failed applicants appeal adverse decisions they are guided by the very same decided cases and legal precedents as we have mentioned above. The SIA also have a quite obsessive procedure for establishing the real identity of the person to whom they are going to issue a badge. All they'd need on top of that for firearm keepers, shooters and dealers is an office to record validations of security and certificates of competence for the various classes of firearm. A computer and a printer can do most of the rest of the work. As we keep saying, the Driver and Vehicle Licensing Agency already, efficiently, keep track of a lot more vehicles than there are firearms in the country—even if you count in the unregistered pool, antiques, museum collections and airguns—and they handle all the driving licence holders too. So we know it can be done.

The SIA is already independent, accountable and steered by the law. It would need to have competently written guidance (the 2002 Home Office guidance is appalling: you have only to read the bit about revoking dealerships to see that it bears no relation whatever to what the Act says). A new Firearms Act would set up an independent appeals process, possibly including a tribunal (a bench of lawyers, *not* bureaucrats) for 'administrative' cases. Actual crimes would remain the province of the courts, but they'd no longer include dealers making minor errors in their record-keeping or shooters being prosecuted for having a couple of rounds over their permitted limit. Come to think of it, that bit of gratuitous interference can get the heave-ho too.

CHAPTER FIFTEEN

CRIME AND PUNISHMENT

T
HE QUESTION naturally arises as to what sanctions should be applied to people who break the rules. Rule-breakers there are, because currently the Firearms Acts create 'absolute offences'. This means that the offence is proven by the facts, not by what you thought and not at all by whether you had any dishonest intention when you broke the rule. So if that American Civil War-era cap and ball revolver by Tucker and Sherrard that you bought as a genuine antique turns out to be an Italian reproduction that some faker has aged with battery acid, the person holding it when the music stops has no defence in law. This seems to us somewhat inconsistent with the principles of natural justice.

Take another example. In 1987, to remain within the section 2 classification, a shotgun barrel had to measure 24 inches or more. At that time, shotguns with barrels that short or shorter were usually repeaters, which have a longer receiver and thus a greater total length than doubles with longer barrels. If it matters. It did matter, of course, if a gunsmith had a burst gun in for repair and, when he'd finished, the barrels were no longer quite long enough. That was nature's way of telling him to scrap the gun and sell the idiot who damaged it a replacement, but it did not always occur to dealers to check their work with a tape measure. An absolute offence, with no grounds of appeal, would be committed by whoever had the gun when the police thoughtfully checked the length of the barrels.

This kind of thing has generated a lot of court cases over the years, particularly when the legislation has been hurriedly drafted and ambiguously worded. The 1988 Act's phrase 'rifle includes carbine' comes to mind. That insinuated itself into the legislation because Douglas Hogg, the Tory Minister who steered the Bill through Parliament, wanted to ban Uzi pistols on the grounds that he thought them ugly (*sic*). Uzi made a small-frame semi-automatic pistol and a large frame—let's use the 'C' word—carbine, although Uzi didn't call it that. These were chambered for 9mm or .45ACP pistol ammunition, and came with either a detachable wooden shoulder stock or a folding metal stock. The latter variant was essentially a semi-auto version of their 1949 submachine gun, and that's what Mr Hogg objected to—it looked like a submachine gun.

What it looked like was one thing, but otherwise (and as defined by the Act), it was a large-frame pistol with a shoulder stock, taking pistol ammunition in a detachable magazine. The magazines came in three capacities—20, 25 and 32 rounds. With the largest magazine it was technically not very different from a First World War-vintage 'artillery' Luger pistol. They shared similar barrel lengths, detachable stocks and a 32-round magazine. The first draft of the revised guidance to police in 1989 said that the prohibition was not intended to catch Luger pistols but *was* intended to catch the Uzi 'carbine', a product that, as far as the manufacturer was concerned, did not exist.

Did someone say that the law is a mess?

So now we had a shambles in the guidance as well as in the law. We don't know if Hogg was simply trying to protect the Treasury from having to dole out a bit more compensation to those who would have given up these guns along with their semi-auto rifles.* So much more satisfying to harass shooters who thought they had acquired weapons legally, by prosecuting them (and their dealers) in their innocence, after the event. It's possible too that the Home Office didn't want to be very clear about what the ban caught, for fear that stating a precise break-point would lead to the trade building guns to the edge of it. Fear comes naturally to bureaucrats; building to legally-set specifications comes naturally to the engineers.

In any case, it is bizarre that the aesthetic proclivities of neurotics should have come anywhere near an Act of Parliament or its associated guidance (Mr Hogg later became quite famous for an expensive obsession with keeping his moat clean and tidy). But it's not atypical of the mess that is current firearms legislation in the UK. On the one hand we have muddles like this, inserted for one ulterior motive or

---

* A legalized-theft scheme was eventually approved by Parliament, but it paid out only half the value of the firearms handed in, and nothing at all for the dedicated accessories. At £150 per rifle, government figures suggest they actually paid out on less than 5,000 of the weapons that the legislation added to section 5. That's about 10 percent of what was out there. Which goes to show that, where firearms are concerned, the government's compliance rate is no better than the public's. Many claims, including ours, have never been settled.

another, and on the other we have absolute—'administrative'—offences that take no account of how or why they occur, and allow no defence in terms of intent (*mens rea*) and no appeal, but are still criminal offences. That has to change.

Make the law simple, civilized, and flexible

Some offences that are currently 'absolute' could remain so, but they should be decriminalized. When Douglas Hurd was prosecuted for possessing a shotgun without a certificate, he had no defence in law. His old shotgun certificate had expired and he had not applied for a new one—so, bang to rights. There was no certificate in force, and none in the pipeline. That was his fault, plain and simple. Late paperwork usually attracts a fixed penalty these days, and so it should be under a new Firearms Act. But even in apparently open-and-shut cases like this there may be mitigating circumstances—such as a man in a coma following a car crash, and his family being unaware of the precarious status of his ticket until the penalty notice flops through the door. A new Act would have to include some mechanism for sorting out that kind of circumstance justly and fairly.

Another currently 'absolute' offence occurs when a firearm certificate holder has more ammunition than his certificate allows. Firearms certificates today authorize the holder to possess a set amount, such as 1500 rounds, and to acquire up to 1200 rounds at a time. These allowances are arbitrary, and police forces are inconsistent in dishing them out. They were suggested in the 1969 guidance as limits for target shooters, although many certificates authorized smaller quantities and a few allowed more. Our view is that any restriction on ammunition holdings should be based on what the security can hold. If it all fits in the cabinet, fine, but if there's a stack of extra on the bedroom floor and Mr Plod spots it, problem. Easily dealt with by a fixed-penalty notice and surrender of the surplus (which would also make the punishment proportionate to the degree of stupidity).

Of passing interest to the really picky is the serial number on the firearm that doesn't exactly match what appears on the certificate. That can happen for a number of reasons, ranging from a dyslexic dealer to a worn number being a matter of opinion, to the simple truth that many older firearms have more than one number on them. Take a Lee Enfield rifle as an example. The Short Magazine Lee Enfield, 1903-18, came with the number stamped in four places—on the receiver, the bolt, the nose cap and the barrel. Some rifles would have had barrels replaced over time, so the barrel number might be different when we see it. To replace the barrel means taking the nosecap off, so it's possible for a unit armourer to dismantle a dozen rifles and then not match the nosecaps to the original weapons as he re-assembles them. Bolts can be lost, and replaced or changed if need be to adjust the headspace, and so forth.

The 'correct', unchanging number is the one on the receiver, if it's legible. At the back of police minds is the thought that if the rifle in possession is not as described on the certificate, then it might be being possessed off-ticket—a nice opportunity for an easy prosecution. In our proposed system, no such opportunity would arise, since the virtual identity of the rifle has the right number. Such anomalies as there are in the case of a particular firearm (such as its Farsi numbering) can be dealt with by additional notes on the virtual file. Straightening things out is better than making criminals out of everyone; while, when it occurs, real negligence should have a fixed price.

Antiques: once more, police and pen-pushers flout the law

Things get more complicated when all is not what it seems. The trickiest area of concern since 1968 has been establishing where the break points fall between sections 1, 2 and 5, and between any section and antique status. What the current Act says is that nothing in it applies to any antique firearm *possessed solely as a curiosity or ornament*. So to define something as an antique means it has to pass two tests. It first has to have been kept as a curiosity or ornament—in a cupboard or on display, but not loaded and under the bed.

Once it's passed the first test, the second is a question of age, and at this point the Home Office guidance is at odds with case law. The Court of Appeal considered antique firearms in *Richards v. Curwen* (1977 3 ALL ER 426). The prosecution argued, *inter alia*, that the exhibits (early marks of .455 Webley revolvers) could not be regarded as antiques because they were less than 100 years old and took 'modern' cartridges—of which production had ceased in 1942. The Court thought that a fixed cut-off date wouldn't work. Antique status was a mix of possession of a bygone, as a curiosity, by someone with a demonstrable interest, such as through other elements of his collection. The court also rejected the ammunition argument. But the Home Office can't let a good theory go to waste, so it's still being used in their guidance. Here you'll also find that some firearms made as long ago as 1855 are regarded as 'modern', while some made as recently as 1939 are 'antique'. Home Office logic, there's nothing like it.

So if you follow the Court of Appeal's views in *Richards v. Curwen*, any firearm possessed as a curiosity or ornament and over about 78 years old is an antique. Two other cases should be mentioned here, though: in R. *v. Howells* (1977 QB 614) the defendant thought that he had an antique cap and ball revolver, but as a matter of fact it turned out to be a modern reproduction. The court held that only the true facts were relevant. Beliefs, albeit honestly and reasonably held, were not a defence. In *Bennett v. Brown* (1980 Cr App R 109) his 1886-type Lebel rifle was held to be an antique, but his 1905 and 1910 pistols were not. Juries like giving a bit to each side.

The trouble is that there's a lot at stake now. If your P08 Luger pistol, made in 1911, is an antique, congratulations: it's worth quite a bit. But if the police prosecute you for possessing it as a 'prohibited small firearm' and your lawyers forget to get competent expert evidence in your defence, it's worth five years. Mandatory. That's because the case turns on the facts as found by the court. Your opinion doesn't count for anything. What *you* think doesn't matter. What the prosecution thinks does.

So should it? All the issues around *possession* that create absolute offences should be dealt with by way of fixed penalty notices, and once again they should not be absolute to the extent of allowing no appeal. There is no point hauling old ladies to court to cop a five-year term for possessing some long-dead ancestor's service revolver. That wouldn't happen if guidance to the police was competent. Inevitably there will always be some cut-off between antique and modern, and that will always to some extent be an arbitrary break, depending on individual cases. So there will always be people holding family heirlooms on both sides of such a rolling break point. Having a system that encourages people to register their heirlooms in order to keep them (and without vandalizing the guns by deactivation) is one way of helping to keep people on the right side of a shifting point of law. But as the parson's wife said to him, "If it wasn't for the Devil, you'd be out of a job!" And so it is with criminals and the police.

It gets better: our way is cheaper

In 2002, the *Shepherd* case confirmed that administrative convictions, such as for having a firearm without the correct category of certificate, don't stigmatize you as a 'danger to public safety or the peace', so all that cost to the taxpayer was rather pointless. In our view, once dealer registrations cover everything and certificate holders can buy whatever they have been trained to use (and keep what's been in the family for generations), the government will save a small fortune on administration. There will be errors, however; fixed penalty notices that could be appealed would be the way to deal with them.

Prosecutions for adminstrative offences tend to result in comparatively small financial penalties for certificate holders where there is no dishonesty involved, but much expense of time and tax-payers' cash. Breaching a certificate condition, for example, costs about £100, as does possessing excess ammunition. Dealers' infringements tend to cost a bit more, around double the fine to individuals for errors on the register and in transactions. We think that fixed penalties would be the slick way to go because, apart from other advantages, they would save so much in court time and expenses. Police would issue them when their investigations discover apparent errors. The recipient would have a right of appeal, probably to the certificate-issuing authority in the first instance. Then the efficacy of the police work can be checked, and an independent body becomes accountable when it imposes or modifies a penalty.

Separation of powers: why our current law is illegal

Revoking certificates should certainly remain a option for a court when a 'danger to public safety or the peace' is proven; that means proven, not imagined. The courts already have the power to cancel certificates on conviction and should be invited to do so when the nature of a conviction suggests that it might be appropriate. In many cases past, the court couldn't impose cancellation because the police had already acted pre-emptively, outside their powers (*ultra vires*), from their own conviction, so to speak. Revocation should be a court matter, not a police device.

We make this last point because, under European legislation and case law and the Human Rights Act, the issuing authority cannot also be the revoking authority, as it is under the current Firearms Acts. But if issuing certificates were centralized, the police could retain the power to suspend (but not revoke) certificates in cases where the matter is sufficiently pressing to warrant immediate action. In such instances, there should be an early review of the police decision, perhaps by a judge, who can weigh the police's reasoning against what the law says and how the courts of record have interpreted it. That should happen within 21 days at most.

As things are, the police have an unacceptably free hand, and not infrequently abuse the privilege. Quite a few businesses have been closed and individual certificates revoked, only to be followed by acquittal on whatever charges the police have scraped up. In the event of what they refer to as a 'failed prosecution', the police tend not to regard the court's decision as final, don't reinstate certificates, and then insist on defending their original decision if appealed. The trouble with all that, apart from the sulky arrogance it reveals, is that the judge sitting in a Crown Court hearing such an appeal, is sitting in the shoes of the chief constable and substituting his decision for that of the chief constable. This is hardly fair and impartial, and on the face of it falls foul of the European Court of Human Rights' decision in *McGonnell v. United Kingdom* (2000). These Star-Chamber practices need to be shovelled out and replaced with an appeal system that is transparent and just—and that complies with the rest of the law.

There are degrees of wickedness

We think that when a conviction rings bells because the offence suggests there may be a 'danger to public safety or the peace', the individual's certificate should be cancelled, with leave to re-apply after a period of calm. This should not exceed 12 months in the first instance, unless the penalty on conviction demands a longer period of disqualification. The court should decide on this, and should have the option of full cancellation, or cancellation only of the authority to possess. That would leave the shooter's basic fit-person certificate intact, thus allowing him to continue practising with borrowed firearms under qualified supervision.

When a prosecution is pending, of course, nobody has a conviction to weigh in the balance, just an accusation—which half the time comes to nothing. In such instances the preservation of public safety is the responsibility of magistrates, not the police. Magistrates can remand a suspect to custody, or bail a suspect with conditions that restrict his access to his hobby or business. Ensuring that *only* magistrates have such discretion will help to ensure that an accused person who's subsequently acquitted won't be deprived of their personal property or their livelihood without due process.

We have the impression that at the back of what we have now is some low-grade politics. While honest people are trying to use firearms legally, the police are using highly questionable administrative powers to try to prevent that. It is not overtly a government policy, but it seems to be a police one. We suspect it's based on their need to generate statistics that show they are 'doing something'—that they are necessary. And yes, they are necessary—just superfluous, and too often pernicious, and mostly unconstitutional, when it comes to the civilized administration of firearms law.

CHAPTER SIXTEEN
BULLET POINTS

T HIS IS our prescription for issuing firearm certificates: a fit-person certificate, validation of security, and certificates of competence for each class (or sub-category, where appropriate) of firearm sought. The complete document should be issued by an accountable, national body. And below, in summary, is the core of our strategy for restoring firearms law—and shooting itself—in the UK to full health and strength:

• Local police firearms management teams to be replaced by one national certification authority, which also will maintain a national database of firearms and transactions.

• The three categories of firearms in the 1968 Act to become one—firearms being defined, as now, as lethal barrelled weapons from which any shot, bullet or missile can be discharged. Non-lethal defence equipment such as pepper sprays (the absolute business for hostile dogs, every postman should carry one) and battery-operated stun 'guns' should be down-graded and thus available to every fit person certificate holder.

• People wanting to take up shooting initially apply to the national authority for a fit-person certificate. This is determined by criminal record and medical checks and is renewable periodically

• The fit-person certificate authorizes the holder to
—join any club that will have him,
—take any firearms training course available to him, and
—borrow guns from firearms certificate holders to use under their supervision.

• Any person passing an appropriate course is entitled to a certificate of competence with a particular class of firearm.

• A fit person holding a certificate of competence may have it translated by the issuing authority into a firearm certificate, provided their storage arrangements have been certified as adequate. The firearm certificate will be valid for five years from the date of translation. Holders must re-certify in each class of firearms for which they seek continued authority, before applying to renew the certificate.

- The rules for a collector are much the same: fit person certificate, certificate of competence, qualifying on a safe handling course, and adequate storage.
- The firearm certificate will authorize the holder to acquire and keep as many firearms as the storage certificate authorizes in the categories in which he or she has demonstrated competence, and as much ammunition as the storage will accommodate.
- The firearm certificate authorizes the holder to allow his firearms to be used in his presence by any fit-person certificate holder.
- The firearm certificate authorizes the holder to take temporary possession of any firearm that he or she thinks may not be on the national database, in order to regularize its status.
- There should be no lower age limit for a fit-person certificate. In practice, there will probably be a common-sense lower limit based on size, strength and maturity that will be individually determined by parents, mentors and instructors.
- The firearm certificate will be in 'credit card' format with the photo of the holder showing, but all other details accessible only through the card reader, for security reasons. The card reader will enable its operator to access all the other information in the certificate holder's file.
- All transactions for which the firearm certificate is required, to be conducted through the card reader and national database. Transactions between certificate holders will have to be conducted through a dealer unless the database management determines an alternative method, such as by telephone.
- Dealers should obtain a fit-person certificate and complete a training course for registration as well as providing adequately insured, secure premises and a business plan to show their intentions.
- Registration as a dealer to include authority to possess any firearm within the meaning of the Act, sections 1, 2 and 5 of the 1968 Act having been amalgamated.
- Shipments between dealers to be notified to national database so that there is monitoring of shippers; any common carrier to be able to bid for the work.
- Dealer's servants should hold individual fit-person certificates.
- Cancellation or revocation of certificates to be ordered only by a court, and only when a danger to public safety or the peace is proven.

- Firearms confiscated on revocation or cancellation to be stored safely and securely, and if a court deems the revocation permanent, compensation at current market value must be paid.
- Certificates may be suspended on medical grounds by the issuing authority on the advice of medically qualified personnel, for the duration of a course of treatment.
- Registration of any firearm for the first time by any person acts as their personal authority to possess it, pending acquisition of full authority to keep it. If disposal is preferred, such as by an executor, documentation will then exist with which to take the firearm into the trade, or for an inheritor to take possession of it through a fit person certificate.
- Registration would require taking the firearm to a dealer or other premises with a terminal so that the firearm can be registered on the national database. Registration must be undertaken by someone who can describe the firearm accurately.
- Police officers should obtain a fit-person certificate prior to undertaking firearms training.
- Police firearms courses should lead to a certificate of competence for successful participants, in the classes of firearm with which they have trained.
- Concealed firearms may be carried by graduates of suitable self-defence courses without them holding a firearm certificate if the firearm is issued by an appropriate body. A firearm certificate will be required to purchase firearms privately for this purpose.
- The 'good reason' for any individual applying for a fit person certificate and taking any training is a matter for the individual.
- Overseas visitors bringing firearms to the UK will need to apply for temporary authority to possess them as an adjunct to their passport, which provides the photo ID element.

And finally

We don't think our proposals represent any slackening of the controls that have built up over time, or that they will have any negative effect on public safety. What we have tried to do is rationalize those controls, weed out the job-creation schemes that have built up over the years, and leave a system that keeps track of authorized persons and their firearms while maintaining a high level of security.

Much of the administration of firearms law in recent times has been aimed at keeping (or getting) people out of the system who would actually prefer to be legal. It's only the law-abiding whose lives are messed around, which is surely coming at the subject from the wrong angle. It has certainly made plenty of work for bureaucrats, but it's achieved little else. After all, none of their efforts has come anywhere near dealing with people with unregistered firearms. Our view is that the more guns are registered, and the easier it is to register them, the more control there is over them. History shows that every time there's an attempt to reduce the number of 'legal' guns in circulation, a huge proportion of previously-registered weaponry disappears off the radar. Our system would reverse that trend.

Most of the rest of our current gun controls have taken decisions that should be made in club committees, in dealerships and syndicates out of the shooting communities, and put them in the hands pf police offices or the Home Office. That has proven to be flawed. The common link between the Hungerford, Dunblane and Whitehaven killers is that responsibility for judging their suitability to have guns rested with remote government employees, not with their peers.

If the registration and certificate-issuing system is national, and the local system of social controls that existed through clubs and dealerships before big government intervened is restored, the shooting sports will help in regenerating the national economy. The people who represent our nation in the Olympics will be the best our country has to offer. And those who want to make our country unpleasant to live in by pursuing an unpatriotic agenda should start to be afraid, because they will not be able to continue in their unlawful ways in the safety they have recently enjoyed.

DRIVING THROUGH MYTHICAL AMERICA

A S WE HAVE OBSERVED from time to time in this book, there is an organization in the UK called the Gun Control Network (hereafter GCN) which, unlike a number of more than somewhat better-qualified experts from the UK's so-called 'gun lobby', has twice been called to give oral evidence on firearms law to the Home Affairs Select Committee of the House of Commons, once in 2000 and again in 2010. The GCN's mission statement, as published on its website, includes this assertion: "All our activities and objectives are predicated on the belief that the interests of public safety demand a reduction in the availability and attractiveness of firearms of all kinds. No reasonable person doubts the fundamental connection between the number of guns there are in a society and the prevalence of gun homicide, suicide and accident." Although the words do not say so, the *implication* here is that the fewer guns there are at large in a society, the fewer people will be murdered.

One doesn't have to look very far to find 'reasonable persons' alive today who would dispute that assertion with some vigour, as well as some rather distinguished dead ones—such as the sober American colonists who wrote the amendments to the US Constitution known as the Bill of Rights. There are, too, plenty of perfectly rational people, not all of them Americans, who would argue that the *more* guns there are in lawful hands, the *less* crime there is likely to be. Reasonable people, in other words, can accept that others may take differing views of the same question.

However, to argue that widespread gun ownership and the routine carrying of firearms helps to keep crime levels down isn't quite the opposite of the claim that fewer guns in society reduces the "prevalence of gun homicide, suicide and accident". Both positions, we would argue, represent an unsophisticated reading of the data—when, indeed, any data has been adduced. The GCN is not notorious for producing its own research papers, although it does cite two particularly thoroughly-discredited papers, by Professors Thomas Gabor and Martin Killias, on its website. Gabor is quoted from his evidence to the Cullen Enquiry: "Homicide rates tend to be related to firearm ownership levels. Everything else being equal, a reduction in the percentage of households owning firearms should occasion a drop in the homicide rate." Such facts as are available suggest that things are much more complex than that.

Guns make you gloomy?

The first thing to tip out of the GCN's litany is suicide. From Durkheim (*Le Suicide*, 1897) on, sociologists and psychologists have observed that a determined would-be suicide will use whatever means are at hand to achieve self-destruction. Drowning, drug overdoses, opening veins or arteries with knives and razorblades, hanging oneself, getting in the way of speeding trains—all are readily available in modern industrial societies, and far more easily attempted in the UK than shooting oneself. Personal experience of people with suicidal tendencies, one of whom attempted three of the above options, suggests to us that the academic literature is accurate. It seems highly unlikely that easy access to firearms would raise the *general* level of suicide in any given *milieu*.

One may also argue back and forth as to whether would-be suicides should be regarded as free to take their own lives or should be strenuously discouraged from so doing. Part of that argument might include whether a 'gesture', or 'cry for help' is made needlessly irrevocable through access to a gun. In our experience, those truly intent on self-destruction choose irremediable ways and means; those less concentrated leave clues, open doors, and other hints that their attempt is more an advertisement than a settled ambition.

Next, let's deal with accidents. Accidents happen: that's a fact of life, as anyone can attest who's tripped over a passing cat when carrying a pail of slops, or who's been skidded into by a passing car on a snowy road. Accidents involving firearms happen because people forget or ignore their training, or become over-confident and careless, or because they have never been trained properly in the first place to treat potentially lethal weapons with proper respect. Even then, things can go wrong. The antidote, surely, is rigorous training—to the point of indoctrination—as early in life as possible in handling guns safely, with regular reminders and refreshers from then on.

Those lucky enough to be bilingual would say the same about their acquaintance with languages.

Personally, we have never forgotten our Dad's uncompromising law that even our light-alloy, fake six-shooter cap-gun, first wielded at about age six, should never be pointed at anyone (not even the cat) to whom we wished no harm. One might draw the moral from this that even toys can be used to inculcate good and lasting habits. And it shows that there is no substance whatever to the idea that public safety and the Queen's peace can be best maintained by restricting firearms training to people over the age of 18 (or any other arbitrary age limit). The earlier people learn how to handle firearms, the better. Just as the earlier they learn a foreign language, the better.

Fewer guns, fewer deaths?

That leaves us with the question of homicide: murder, to you and me. Deliberate, unlawful killing. With a gun.

The GCN insists, in so many words, that there is a "fundamental connection" between the prevalence of guns in society and the prevalence of homicide with guns. The factoid usually invoked to support this position is that the United States has 'lax' gun-control laws, and look what happens there—people are riddled with bullets every day of the week, Sundays not excluded. To its credit, the GCN doesn't haul this particular indigestible chestnut out of its fire, but it does have a page on its website that purports to show what dire straits the US is in.

Meanwhile, it needs to be said for the benefit of those with no direct experience of the US—and those who haven't bothered to look any deeper than the broadest of facts—that gun-control laws there are anything but uniform, and some are extremely stringent. Federal law tends to focus on fully automatic weapons and, the bugbear of all gun-control advocates, handguns: which is to say semi-automatic pistols, and revolvers. Federal law requires licensed dealers to run a background check, via the FBI, on would-be handgun buyers to ensure that they are not felons, convicted drug addicts, guilty of domestic violence, mentally ill, fugitives from justice, illegal aliens, and so on. Fully automatic weapons are not illegal or banned in the US, but to own them you have to demonstrate that you're an unimpeachably respectable citizen, and then pay the Federal government a handsome fee for the privilege. Anyone else, such as those of the Mafia-footsoldier, violin-case-wielding variety, risks being clobbered by the law. Since the end of Prohibition in 1933, even unregistered full-auto weapons have rarely—albeit on occasion spectacularly—

been used in crime, less because of the law than because for most armed criminals they're not a practical option.

Handgun laws are another matter. Americans are rather in favour of keeping controls of anything in local hands, be it parking restrictions or water rights: so, unless specifically exempted, State laws can be overridden by County laws, and City laws or local ordinances can overrride both. As a result there are, it's said, some 20,000 gun control laws in force across the US, and people who like to travel widely in the country and take their guns with them have much homework to do before firing up their RV (with sunken Roman tub, air conditioning and GPS) and heading off to rough it in the wide blue yonder. In addition, Federal law also obliges gun-carrying citizens to avoid designated 'gun-free' zones, which for example extend 100 feet in all directions beyond the limits of a school's grounds. This is where the GPS may come in handy. Even then, local law can override Federal law by providing certain conditions in which firearms may, for example, be brought onto school grounds (usually, basically, requiring weapons to be unloaded and made not instantly accessible). How many people actually observe such ordinances is anyone's guess. In our recent experience, those who habitually go armed are also aware of the Columbine killings and similar episodes, and don't strive too officiously to put obstacles in the way of a rapid response should the grim occasion arise.

This is all grist to the mill of what personal, easily-portable firearms are actually for, but not to the general point we are heading toward. And that is, that American States with very similar, and by British government standards very 'lax', gun-control laws may show very different statistics when it comes to murder rates *per se*. The two examples we will look at closely are Vermont in New England, on the Canadian border, and New Mexico in the Southwest, on the Mexican border. According to a 2001 survey, the two States have roughly comparable levels of gun ownership—42 percent of households in Vermont, and about 35 percent of households in New Mexico.

North East versus South West

Vermont has precisely two gun-control laws. One (apart from reiterating Federal law) calls for dealers to keep records of their transactions, prohibits sales of guns to anyone under the age of 16 (fine: $10 to $50), pointing loaded guns at people ($50 fine) or firing at them (up to a year in jail or $100 fine) except in self-defence or the line of duty. Vermont also prohibits carrying a firearm "with the intent or purpose of injuring another", which clearly excludes carrying for self-defence or any other lawful purpose. Vermont does not require firearms to be registered with the State, and does not prohibit anyone from carrying a loaded weapon in public, whether it's visible or concealed. In 2009 Vermont had a murder rate of 1.1 per 100,000 head of population, which compares nicely with league-topper Pennsylvania, which that year suffered over 36 murders per 100,000 head. Since 1960, Vermont's ratio has never gone above 5.5 and has been as low as 0.3/100,000. The average for the years 1960 to 2009 is 2.08, which is fractionally above the rate for England and Wales, which runs at about 1.8/100,000.

The lack of gun controls in Vermont would not, then, appear to encourage people to slaughter one another. The mild sentences, even for shooting at someone with aggressive intent, would seem to reflect the State legislators' presumption that most people, most of the time, wouldn't do that sort of thing: and if things go seriously wrong, other statutes will take care of the consequences. Murder by firearm is still murder; the *means* to homicide are not demonized in Vermont law.

New Mexico has similar, if slightly less relaxed attitudes to firearms ownership. As in Vermont, there is no official registry of who owns what gun or how many of them, and carrying a concealed, loaded firearm is legal on one's own property. New Mexico's doctrine of 'extended domain' means that one may also carry a concealed, loaded weapon in one's car. To carry a firearm in public, one must either carry the weapon openly—as some do—or, if concealed, either carry it unloaded or have qualified for a concealed-carry permit. However, carrying concealed in public without a permit is deemed a petty misdemeanour and attracts a $5 (*sic*—five dollar) fine. Firearms are not permitted in bars, loaded or otherwise (a fourth-degree felony), but may be taken into restaurants whose sales of alcohol represent less than 60 percent of turnover, provided the owner of the premises has no objection.

The general murder rate on the other hand is far higher in New Mexico than in Vermont, running at an average of 9.03/100,000 over the years 1960–2009. In that time it has never dropped below 5.4/100,000, while 1975 saw a high of 13.3. From 2005 to 2009 inclusive, the average has been 7.74/100,000, somewhat above the US's national rate, which generally hovers between 6 and 7/100,000.

One might speculate that New Mexico's high murder rate, compared with Vermont's, is not unconnected to its proximity to Mexico, with various back roads being used to run drugs across the border, and associated trade wars. Attractive as this idea is, we have no data to support it.

The vexed question of ethnicity

What we can point to is the huge disparity in the ethnic make-up of the two states. Vermont's population is about 95 percent white, with Afro-Americans, Hispanics and Asians making up most of the rest. More than 86 percent of the population has a high-school diploma. In contrast New Mexico's population is roughly 42 percent Hispanic, 10 percent American Indian, 2.5 percent Afro-American, and most of the rest are white. Albuquerque's population is about 30 percent Mexican-American. About 27 percent of the population has a high-school diploma. Before someone squawks about any outrageous assumptions being made here, consider some more statistics.

As of 2000, in the US as a whole, the homicide rate for non-Hispanic whites was 2.8/100,000, that for Hispanics 8.3, and that for blacks 22.4. In other words, the black rate is eight times the white rate, with the Hispanic rate very nearly three times the white rate. In New Mexico in 2006, murder rates by ethnicity, per 100,000 of population, were reported by the NM Department of Health (in round figures) to be: Afro-American–22; American Indian–15; Hispanic–12; white–5. Proportions are different, but one can see that the general pattern nationwide is echoed in these figures.

We don't profess any competence in assessing *why* these disparities exist or why they are so vast, although the words 'alcohol' (for American Indians) and 'drugs' are bound to enter any speculation. It's worth closing this segment with the observation that in 2004/5, at least, fewer than 50 percent of homicides in New Mexico were committed with a firearm, despite their ready availability.

Pack 'em in and pile 'em high

In any case, an essential fact to bear in mind in this discussion is that the US is, overall, a far more violent society than the UK, in the particular sense that a much higher proportion of the population—historically, about five times as many—are prepared to murder their fellow citizens, for whatever reason. (The UK does however lead the US in rates of other violent crime as well as in robbery and burglary.) The second essential fact to note is that high murder rates in the Western world are associated with high population density: both US and UK cities show a far higher incidence of murder than do rural areas. New Mexico has vast, thinly populated areas of mountain, desert and prairie, but more than 50 percent of its population is concentrated in three centres: the capital Santa Fe (pop. 73,000), Las Cruces (95,000), Albuquerque (530,000; the city's metropolitan area houses 870,000 people, nearly half the population of the entire State).

Writing in the Albuquerque *Journal* in March 2008, when New Mexico appeared, statistically, to be the 'third most dangerous state' in the Union, professional risk assessor Madison D. Link observed: "In New Mexico's rural areas, the murder rate is slightly above the US average, at 6.08 per 100,000 persons. The Albuquerque metropolitan area (Valencia, Bernalillo and Sandoval counties) has a rate of 10.4 per 100,000 persons. This is actually typical for a metropolis of our size. Nashville, Tenn., San Francisco and Louisville, Ky., are three cities of similar size and similar murder rates."

In contrast, Vermont's one major city and its capital, Burlington, is home to around 39,000 people—about four fifths the number who live in the UK's sleepy cathedral city of Salisbury, Wiltshire. The entire population of Vermont amounts to a little over 620,000 souls, spread over 9,600 square miles. Albuquerque has 85 percent of that number of people, 570,000 of them, tucked into 181 square miles—45 times as many humans per square mile. It would be foolish to say that high population density *causes* a high rate of murder, but there does appear to be a correlation between the *size* of a community, its population density, and its levels of violence.

We *can* say more firmly that Vermont and New Mexico, which are broadly comparable in the lack of restriction they place on their residents' owning and carrying firearms—notably handguns—present a striking contrast in their respective incidence of murder. And that that correlates with an equally striking difference in demographics. In the context it's not particularly cheering to observe that murder tends to be contained within ethnic groups—that is, when for instance Afro-Americans murder, they usually kill other Afro-Americans.

The view from elsewhere

Looking at what happens in a number of other US States and cities is also revealing. According to the FBI, in 2007—whose figures are the most comprehensive we have to hand—some 14,180 people were murdered in the US, of whom about 8,500 were shot. North Dakota, which has no firearms registration or licensing in place, saw three people unlawfully killed, none of them with a gun; two victims were knifed, and one was a bare-hand killing. This in a State where nearly 51 percent of households have a gun. Wyoming, with almost identical gun laws and where nearly 60 percent of households have firearms, had 10 murders; four of the victims were shot. Twelve people were murdered in New Hampshire, which has very similar firearms laws to New Mexico's; only two died by gunfire. Thirty percent of New Hampshire households own firearms.

In contrast, consider the three States that topped the 2007 murder league. Illinois, with guns in 20 percent of households, had 530 homicides, 421 (nearly 80 percent) of them shootings. Louisiana, with guns in 44 percent of homes, had 390 murders, including 309 shootings (nearly 80 percent). Missouri, where 42 percent of households have firearms, saw 455 murders, 349 (77 percent) of them committed with a gun. Let's look at these States in more detail.

Murder-plagued Illinois is not a gun-friendly State. It operates a complicated and laborious system of firearm registration and permits, and includes Chicago which, from 1982 until 2010, banned handgun purchase and registration entirely, although those who had already owned registered guns were allowed to keep them. (In 2010, the landmark McDonald case in the US Supreme Court allowed city residents to keep handguns at home for self-defence.) Neither general State regulations nor the local handgun ban prevented 379 Chicagoans being murdered with firearms in 2009—nearly 83 percent of a total of 458 homicides. Admittedly, this was less than half the total of 943 murders the city had seen in 1992—a rate of 34 per 100,000 head of population; but that 1992 figure represented a more-than 17 percent increase on 1982, when the handgun ban became law in order, supposedly, to improve public safety. To labour the obvious: Chicago's draconian gun-control laws clearly had no effect on general levels of homicide in the city, and none on the proportion of them committed with firearms.

Louisiana includes New Orleans, long among the top three US cities for murder of all kinds; neither the city nor the State has much gun regulation, and under Louisiana law New Orleans cannot pass firearms ordinances that are more restrictive than the State's own.

Missouri includes St Louis and Kansas City, rated the second and third "most dangerous" cities in the US by *Forbes* magazine in 2010; in 2007, St Louis had a murder rate of 39/100,000, outdoing the Chicago of the 1990s by a fair margin; an overwhelming proportion of crime in the city is concentrated in East St Louis, which happens to be one of the poorest and most derelict black ghettos in the country. Missouri has no firearm registration or licensing system and, as in Louisiana, State law forbids local administrations from imposing stricter controls.

Taken together, these three States and the three least violent ones shows no statistical relationship between gun regulation or registration, levels of firearms ownership, or patterns of homicide, with or without firearms.

Tales of two cities

Two US cities that are routinely cited as illustrating the fatuity of gun controls are New York and Washington, D.C. In part a knee-jerk response to an assassination attempt on New York Mayor William Gaynor, the 1911 Sullivan Act effectively outlawed privately-owned pistols in New York City. It is not impossible, but it is difficult and expensive to acquire a handgun permit (which allows concealed carry), and rumour has it that they tend to be issued to the rich, the famous, and the politically well-connected: Donald Trump and Robert de Niro are among the beneficiaries. Of some 30,000 permits on issue, only about 8000 have gone to individuals who are not retired law-enforcement officers. As elsewhere, the law has proved no great restraint to the criminally inclined. A record 2245 murders occurred in New York City in 1990, 69.4 percent of them with a firearm; but this was when old-fashioned Mafia violence was still endemic while, at the same time, young, mainly black, drug-trafficking gangs were on the rise and establishing pecking orders and operational 'turf'. Currently, the city's murder rate per 100,000 head is fractionally below the US national average; in 2007 New York saw 'only' 501 murders, of which 61 percent were committed with a firearm—a firearm that, virtually by definition, was illegally owned.

This reduction in homicide follows a nation-wide trend in falling crime rates—Chicago, as seen above, was part of the same pattern. Similarly, Washington D.C., which had banned private handgun ownership and required registration of rifles and shotguns in 1976, had a peak of 474 murders in 1990 in a population of 606,000-odd—a ferocious 78.2 per 100,000, which earned the city the unenviable soubriquet of "murder capital of the world". The next year was even worse: 482 murders, or 80.6/100,000. By 2009 this had fallen to 144 murders, still four times the national average rate, but still a drop of 70 percent. As in New York and Chicago, the bloodbaths of the 1990s can be laid at the door of gang warfare over drug (mainly crack cocaine)-selling 'rights'; it is not irrelevant to note that Washington was 60 percent black in 1990; today the figure is nearer 55 percent.

Speaking to the Home Affairs Select Committee's enquiry on firearms law in 2010, the District of Columbia's Attorney-General, Peter Nickles, failed to tell the Committee that before before the 1976 handgun ban, Washington's murder rate had actually been declining, whereas by 1991 it had risen by 200 percent, against an overall rise nationally of 9 percent. He also observed rather disingenuously that since Washington had, in 2008, instituted a system of handgun registration, the number of murders involving firearms had fallen. What he didn't say—or, not to put too fine a point on it, lied by omission about—was that in 2008 the city had been obliged by the US Supreme Court to allow residents to keep handguns at home for self-defence; registration was actually a *liberation*, not a tightening, of the *status quo ante.*

It is surely apparent from the statistics noted throughout this essay that it is as simplistic to argue that 'more guns = less crime' as it is to claim that 'gun control = fewer murders'. However, the enormous publicity attendant on the Supreme Court case and the District's change in its law *may* have contributed to the decline in its homicide rate. That is to say—D.C.'s new law *may* have deterred criminals from undertaking armed burglaries, if only because would-be perpetrators could no longer be certain that their potential victims were not among the 1200-odd people who since 2008 have subjected them-selves to D.C.'s labyrinthine and costly registration system and acquired a handgun for home defence.

The psychology of the situation had, after all, been well illustrated years before in Orlando, Florida. In 1966, the incidence of rape had become an embarrassment to the city. Local police offered, and local media publicised, a one-day seminar to teach Orlando women how to use a firearm in self-defence. Only some 4–500 women were expec-ted to turn up for the course, but 2500 showed. Overwhelmed, the police sent them home, but organized a more thorough, three-class course for anyone who wanted to attend. Within six months, more than 6000 women had learned basic self-defence handgun techniques and the relevant law. The number of rapes in Orlando in 1967 was 89 percent lower than it had been the previous year, although not one woman had fired a weapon in self-defence. In the rest of Florida and the US at large, however, rape statistics remained constant. Five years after Orlando's training programme, rape was still below 1966 levels, but had increased by 308 percent in surrounding areas, by 96 percent in Florida overall, and 64 percent across the US.

No licence to kill

Taken together, the figures we've cited with regard to both States and cities in the US show no correlation to murder rates, the number, kind and intensity of official obstacles to obtaining a gun legally, a community's level of firearms ownership—particularly *legal* owner-ship—and the number or extent of homicides by gunfire. States and cities with no gun regulation may show low levels of violence in general, and few firearms-related murders, as often as officially highly regulated jurisdictions may show high levels of murder by shooting—

and *vice-versa*. And there are all shades in between.

Two general conclusions seem logical enough to appeal to any *reasonable person*. First, bureaucratic systems designed to keep firearms out of private ownership have no effect on murder rates; and second, *lack* of regulation or obstruction to possessing firearms is not followed *ipso facto* by high levels of gun-related violence. It is also reasonable to infer, looking between the lines of the statistics, that local conditions—cultural norms, social pressures, ethnicity, levels of and attitudes to crime, poverty, drug availability and so on—have a far greater effect on determining the degree of violence exhibited in any particular community. Magically removing all the firearms from, say, the gangs of the East St Louis ghetto is not going to diminish their members' appalling tendency to slaughter one another, any more than 'banning handguns' in the UK reduced the number of drug-related shootings (*or knifings*) in the years that followed.

Murder will out, guns or no guns

So far, we've been talking about comparative murder rates in general. The Gun Control Network, however, would be justified in objecting that we've ignored their core claim—that the fewer guns there are in society at large, then the fewer "gun homicides", as they put it, would occur. This is not quite what they want people to think, but it is what they say. The case of North Dakota (51 percent of households with guns; no homicides by shooting) in 2007 severely compromises the universality of that argument. But—well, yes: in general, one might agree with the principle that, if no guns *at all*, legal or otherwise, were to be had for love nor money in, say, the Isle of Wight, then such murders as were committed there would indeed not involve guns. They'd simply be effected with something else—bare hands, brass pokers, electric toasters, hammers, kitchen knives, rat poison, bags of frozen lamb chops, or whatever else came to hand.

But are we supposed to think that murdering someone with any of these freely available items is somehow morally superior to shooting them? Or that, no gun being handy, these killings wouldn't have happened?—because that's the logic of the GCN's position. When US citizens kill one another, by the national average they use a firearm in about 60–70 percent of cases. The weapons used may or may not be registered, and may or may not be legally held in any particular jurisdiction. But there *are* a lot of firearms in America: an estimated 300 million of them—a third of them handguns—spread across about 50 million, or 42 per cent of, households. If all those firearms were abducted by aliens overnight, does any *reasonable person* suppose that murder rates in the US would proceed to drop like a concrete pudding into still waters?

A journey into Scotland

Some evidence from elsewhere suggests otherwise. In 2003 Glasgow, Scotland, had the distinction of being dubbed "the murder capital of western Europe" by the press. Official figures showed that in 2002, Glasgow saw 40 people murdered, a rate of 5.87 per 100,000 head of population (more than twice that of London), and representing about 31 percent of all homicides in Scotland. More than half the national total—68 out of 127—were fatal stabbings. "In at least 44 per cent of cases the accused was drunk. In 10 per cent of cases, the accused was on drugs and in 15 per cent of cases, drunk and on drugs," reported *The Independent* of 23 November 2003. The story noted that Glasgow was simultaneously seeing a rise in young street gangs "armed with knives and heavy leather belts", although typically Scottish murder victims were stabbed by friends or relatives, at home. The Scottish Government's bulletin itself records that in 56 percent of cases, the murder was the upshot of a drunken altercation or rage. The figures for 2004 were worse still, with 137 homicides nationwide, although the general circumstances in which they occurred remained much the same.

Only three (2.37 percent) of the 127 murders in 2002 were the result of shooting; in 2004, eight victims (5.8 percent) were shot. The government's bulletins do not say whether the weapons used were registered or not, or whether they were rifles, pistols, or shotguns. We do know that only about 1.2 percent of households in Scotland in those years contained registered firearms, the vast majority of them rifles, which are not the weapon of choice (especially when secure in a cabinet) for anyone in a drunken fury. One might indeed speculate that the number of deaths by shooting might have been higher in Scotland in 2002 and 2004, were firearms more freely available there. But it is *not* legitimate in the face of the evidence to propose that with more guns there would have been more murders overall.

The stronger and more relevant point that Glasgow and Scotland illustrate is that murder, *by whatever means*, does not occur in a social or cultural vacuum. The unpretty truth is that in these years Glaswegians were more drunk more often, and markedly shorter of temper, than Londoners; and, perhaps as a result, were twice as murderous—and in wielding knives to unhealthy effect were five times more murderous than gun-drenched North Dakota's citizens were in 2007.

General conclusions

Overall, in light of the data reviewed here, we would argue that:

- Murders involving firearms should be seen in the context of general levels of violence in any community
- There appears to be a complex relationship between population density, size of community, ethnicity, and local socio-cultural factors, that contributes to a community's propensity to violence
- The number of private firearms in any particular community shows no fixed correlation with *rates* of murder in general
- Levels of private firearms ownership in any particular community have no fixed or predictable correlation with the *proportion* of homicides committed with a firearm
- Systems of firearm registration, licensing, and other bureaucratic impediments to private citizens keeping and bearing arms while going about their lawful occasions have *no discernible effect* on general levels of homicide, *including fatal shootings*, in any given jurisdiction
- Any debate on the usefulness of 'gun controls' should start and end with the best available facts, not the worst available prejudice

Attempts at 'gun control' have always fixated on firearms—inanimate examples of precision engineering and ingenious metallurgy that, by themselves, can do nothing, and that can be used for good, for ill, or just for fun. But ultimately, the old saw that 'guns don't kill people, people kill people', applies. It's not guns or knives or bricks, but human beings who acquire or stumble on the motives, the means and the opportunities to commit violence—as much as to act altruistically (which is probably more often). It is here, with human behaviour, that 'gun control'—which includes responsible firearms ownership—should begin, not with neuroses about unconscious objects and a pathological tendency to risk aversion.

The size of the United States and the variety of socio-cultural norms within it—some sane, grounded and wise; others reckless, rootless and nihilistic—make that nation a potential goldmine of data on homicide and other violent crimes, their causes and contexts. The generally widespread possession of firearms makes the country and its localities particularly susceptible to intelligent research. Similar differences in the relatively un-armed United Kingdom between urban and rural communities, and the more subtle cultural divisions within them, likewise provide a potential treasury of data on the nature of, and attitudes to, justified and unjustified violence.

ACKNOWLEDGEMENTS

Over the years the authors have come to owe much, to many people, for imparting their expertise, scholarly and practical, in firearms. They are too numerous to mention, and we'd probably leave out someone crucial if we tried to compile an inevitably long list: but thanks to you all.

In assembling this polemic, we've been fortunate in being able to pick the brains and mine the extensive researches of Edward Beck and Derek Bernard; Mary Martinek provided data from New Mexico, and John Reuther of the New York Police Department helped with useful statistics. Massad Ayoob has acquainted us with the way of life in New England; Ian Macbeth was an excellent source in Kenya. Ed Beck, Megan J. Davies, and Frank Berry (and his bears) read our manuscript and made many helpful suggestions for improving it. We owe special thanks to Richard Munday who, by way of a felicitous cross-head, provided us with our title.

Throughout the writing, Elizabeth Law has shown extraordinary tolerance and forbearance. Peter Brookesmith is particularly grateful for the many delicious meals she has served him. Especially the roast potatoes.

Lightning Source UK Ltd.
Milton Keynes UK
UKOW050614221211

184228UK00001B/1/P